RETAIN PER CDO

D0393930

TWAYNE'S WORLD AUTHORS SERIES

A Survey of the World's Literature

Sylvia E. Bowman, Indiana University

GENERAL EDITOR

GREECE

Mary P. Gianos, Detroit Institute of Technology

EDITOR

George Theotokas

TWAS 339

George Theotokas

George Theotokas

By THOMAS DOULIS
Portland State University

TWAYNE PUBLISHERS

A DIVISION OF G. K. HALL & CO., BOSTON

Library of Congress Cataloging in Publication Data

Doulis, Thomas.
    George Theotokas.

    (Twayne's world authors series, TWAS 339)
    Bibliography: pp. 173–79.
    1. Theotokas, Giörgos.
PA5610.T5Z6   889'.8'3409   74–14564
ISBN 0–8057–2881–3

AT LONG LAST, THIS BOOK

IS DEDICATED TO

PHAEDON AND STELLA KOZYRIS

Contents

About the Author

Preface

Chronology

About the Author

Thomas Doulis is a novelist, poet, translator and critic. His interest in modern Greek letters has led him to study in depth the impact of the Asia Minor Disaster of 1922 on Greek fiction and the subsequent development and achievements of the Generation of the 1930s, a group of writers who emerged as a response to this traumatic historical event. Much of the research for the present study of George Theotokas was done in Greece during the years 1968–1970 where Doulis was supported by a Fulbright grant.

Doulis has published two novels, *Path for our Valor* (1963) and *The Quarries of Sicily* (1969). His translations from the Greek, primarily of the lyric poetry of Nikiphoros Vrettakos, his criticism, and his own verse have appeared in periodicals like *The American Scholar, Harper's Magazine, Texas Quarterly, The Forum for Modern Language Studies* (Scotland), *Prairie Schooner, Northwest Review, Chicago Review* and *The Virginia Quarterly Review.*

Doulis, associate professor of English at Portland State University in Oregon, is currently writing a novel, revising a number of essays on the significant novelists of the Generation of the 1930s, and collaborating on an introduction to a literature textbook for a major publisher.

Preface

Few writers in most national literatures are able to express
themselves in a variety of genres. Most find their voices in
poetry, fiction, drama, criticism, or scholarship and devote their
exclusive attention to their chosen field, risking their reputations
only occasionally by venturing—out of some compelling need—
into another genre, frequently one associated with their major
field of interest. Those comparatively few writers whose interests
are wide-ranging and whose cultivation of various genres has
led them into questions of intellectual and aesthetic history are
excellent guides to the literature of the nation they represent.
These "men of letters" are part of their time because they register
its controversies and express its certitudes and perplexities.

George Theotokas is such a man. One reads his fiction, his
drama, and his discursive prose—whether journalistic, argumentative, critical, or philosophic—with delight and profit, since
one feels that every statement represents the sincere and considered thought of a fearless, intelligent, and often profound
man. In every expression, Theotokas brought to his work a
deep study, a clarity of mind, and a sense of measure. His essays,
always written for the educated layman, range through history,
sociology, politics, and religion; his travel articles and books are
sensitive and perceptive, while his thoughts on art and literature are always probing and convincing. His drama shows a
technical interest in that weakest of all modern Greek arts and
an achievement that few of his contemporaries were able to
surpass. Since his fiction, which ranges from the short story
through the novella to the large-scale, two-volume novel, was
his main concern, it will be given extended treatment in
this study.[1]

Not having had the honor and the pleasure of knowing George
Theotokas, I am indebted for many details of his life and work

to men and women who gave freely of their time and effort. First of all, I would like to thank Madame Koralia Theotokas for the warm and gracious interest she took in my work, affording me the use of her late husband's study and library and introducing me to people who were able to answer specific questions that came up in the course of my research. Through her auspices I was able to meet the author's sister, Madame Lilika Alevizatos, who provided me with details of Theotokas's early family life and helped round out a picture that had previously been dependent totally on the written word.

George Katsimbalis, who honored me with his friendship for two years, provided me not only with conversation, food, and drink but with a vast fund of information on modern Greek culture that cannot be duplicated in any academy in the world. He and Andreas Karandonis gave me background to the events of the thirties that enabled me to reach certain conclusions about that important post-Disaster decade. Constantine Dimaras, in one short interview, gave me information about, and a perspective on, certain facets of Theotokas's work that would otherwise have taken me months to attain, and Theofilos Frangopoulos supplied me with the insight of a younger contemporary of Theotokas. To my good friend Nikos Avyeris I am indebted for the inclusion of many details and the checking of certain facts that my absence from Greece barred me from doing myself. Professor Mary P. Gianos, editor of the TWAS Greek Authors Series, was full of encouragement during the writing of the study and has done a thorough job on the book while it was still in typescript. I would like to thank Mrs. Kathy Moeller, secretary of the English Department at Portland State University, and the Misses Patricia Knott and Cindy Brown for the care and interest they took in typing a book full of names that must have been incomprehensible to them.

Finally, I'd like to document my profound gratitude to the Institute of International Education for a grant that enabled me to spend 1968–1970 (not the most politically happy years) in Greece. Without the Fulbright grant this book, in particular, and the subsequent studies I hope to complete, would be of limited value. For this I thank the enlightened Federal Administrations that established and maintained the United States Educational

Preface

Foundation in Greece and staffed it with men of the caliber of its Director, James F. Warner, one of the most enlightened and capable administrators it has been my good fortune to encounter.

Thomas Doulis

Portland, Oregon

Chronology

1905   Born in Constantinople, August 14, to Androniki Nomikou and Michael, both of Chios.

1922   The Asia Minor Disaster brings family to Athens where father builds up a fine law practice and represents Greece at the Lausanne Conference. Androniki travels to Constantinople and returns with the private files of the Patriarchate. Theotokas enrolls at the Law School of the University of Athens.

1925   Psycharis in Chios. Theotokas is elected general secretary of the Students' Company (*Foititiki Syndrofia*).

1926   Theotokas is suspended in final year from the university for his activities with the Students' Company. Reinstated. Receives diploma from the university.

1927–   "Free" studies in Paris.
1928

1928   Goes to London in the autumn of 1928. Writes *Elefthero Pnevma* (Free Spirit).

1929   Manuscript of *Free Spirit* is ready in July. Returns to Greece where he publishes *Free Spirit* under the pseudonym of Orestes Digenis.

1931   Begins to practice law in Athens. Publishes *Leisure Hours* and starts contributing to *Kyklos*.

1932   Publishes *Forward to the Social Problem*.

1933   First book of *Argo: The Beginning* is published.

1933–   Founds *Idea* with Spyros Melas and Yiannis Oikonomidis.
1934

1934   *Phylla Imerologiou* (Journal Leaves), poetry collections, published in two installments, the first in April in eighty numbered copies and the second in October in fifty numbered copies.

1935   Founds *Nea Grammata* with Katsimbalis and others.

1936   Definitive version of *Argo* published.

1937   *Euripides Pendozalis and Other Stories* published. Theotokas breaks with *Nea Grammata* group and begins contributing to *Neoellinika Grammata*.

1938   *The Daemon* is published.

1939   Theotokas receives Prose Award of the Academy of Athens and publishes *Journal of Argo and of The Daemon*.

1940   *Leonis* is printed. Italy invades Greece.

1944   Publishes *Theater I*.

1945   Publishes *On the Threshold of a New Era*.

1945–   Is appointed general director of the National Theater of
1946   Greece (February 10, 1945 to May 10, 1946).

1947   Publishes *Theater II*.

1948   Marries Nausicaa, his first wife.

1950   *The Sacred Road* is published, which eventually becomes volume one of *Invalids and Wayfarers*.

1950–   Appointed general director of the National Theater of
1952   Greece for the second time (July 28, 1950 to December 9, 1952).

1953   Travels to the United States.

1954   Publishes *Essay on America*.

1956   Campaigns for office of deputy for the island of Chios and is defeated. Publishes *Problems of Our Time*.

1957   Receives Essay Award from the Greek state.

1958   Publishes *The Price of Freedom* and *Encounter on Pendeli* in separate editions.

1959   *Alcibiades* published in separate edition. Nausicaa dies after long illness.

1960   Travels to the Middle East and to Mount Athos. He discusses the establishment of the National Theater of Northern Greece with Prime Minister Karamanlis.

1961   Presides over the committee for the organization of the National Theater of Northern Greece. Publishes *Journey to Middle East and to Mount Athos* and collects the scattered essays of his lifetime in *Intellectual Journey*.

1963   Publishes *End of the Road* in separate edition. Joins the editorial board of *Epoches*.

1964   Acts as president of the Executive Council of the National Theater from May 6, 1964 to January, 1965. Publishes the definitive edition of *Invalids and Wayfarers*.

Chronology

1965   Receives the Novel Award from the Greek state for *Invalids and Wayfarers* and publishes *Theatrical Works, I: Neoelliniko Laiko Theatro*. After the events of July, he begins writing political articles for *Vima* and resigns from the society of "The Twelve."

1966   Marries the poet, Koralia Andreiadi. Publishes *The National Crisis* and *Theatrical Works, II: Erga Diafora*.

1966   Dies October 30.

CHAPTER 1

The Free Spirit

FAMILY tradition, always an important consideration in Greek culture, is for a number of reasons crucial in the case of George Theotokas. His family hailed from the island of Chios: his father, Michael, from the Pyrgi and his mother, Androniki Nomikou, from Nenita. Throughout his life Theotokas identified certain virtues with the people of the Aegean: they were inclined to moderation in their views and outward behavior; they were simple in their needs and habits, direct and reasonable in discourse, and rational and liberal in orientation; they were not warlike or ostentatious or dogmatic; they were, on the contrary, soft-spoken, friendly, witty, and flexible. They had never, to their honor, provided Greece with a dictator because, Theotokas supposed, they lacked the necessary spiritual and intellectual rigidities that went into the make-up of the totalitarian personality. In characterizing the picture of the Aegean islander that emerges from the fiction, the drama, and the essays of George Theotokas, we seem to have drawn a portrait of the artist himself, a portrait whose authenticity can be attested to by most of the men and women who knew him.

One would not know very much about Theotokas, however, if one ignored two major interests in his life that were kept fairly well submerged by his more obvious concerns for politics and literature. His profound interest in religion, which for him embraced the role of the church in the world as well as the mystical apprehension of a truth unavailable to the rational mind, would have been a surprising development in his later life to someone who did not know the family's religious tradition. His granduncle Germanos Theotokas (?–1918) left the

17

Pyrgi to study at the Great School of the Nation in Constantinople and at the theological schools of Chalkis and of the University of Athens. Ordained at Nea Moni in Chios, he served as a parish priest at the Galata in Constantinople before beginning his rise in the hierarchy that was to culminate in his elevation to the Metropolitan See of Leros and Kalymnos.

The well-drawn Papa Sideros in *Argo*, his first novel, was also, like Germanos, a parish priest in Galata. Though he is the first religious figure to enter the fiction of Theotokas, the concern with the suprarational did not become a significant factor in the novelist's imaginative life until the Occupation years forced him to turn inward to find the sources of good and evil. These were manifested first in his dramatic works, but his major post–World War II novel, *Invalids and Wayfarers*, particularly the second volume, and *The Bells*, his final work, are imbued with a religious apprehension of life.

Besides this interest in religion, which was for obvious reasons identified initially with the city of Constantinople, Theotokas was by training a lawyer, a profession that he had followed in the footsteps of his father, Michael (1872–1951), who was counsel to the Ecumenical Patriarchs Constantine V and Joachim III. Michael Theotokas wrote a number of legal studies relevant to ecclesiastical affairs and the Greek Orthodox community in the Ottoman Empire, and—after the Asia Minor Disaster—acted, at the request of Eleftherios Venizelos, as legal advisor to the Greek Committee at the Conference of Lausanne in 1922–23. It was in this capacity that he drafted the highly important treaty on the exchange of populations.

The legal training of Theotokas does not manifest itself so much as subject matter in his fiction as it does in his approach to the description of reality; it is in the gathering of information, the sifting of evidence, and the dispassionate exposition of his attitudes that one tends to find the influence of his education as a lawyer.

To his granduncle's commitment to religion and his father's orientation toward parliamentary (i.e., Venizelist) liberalism, George Theotokas—besides his lifelong preoccupation with literature—added another highly important commitment, one not evident in either Germanos or Michael: the interest in the demotic language. The Greek of Germanos, as expected, was heavily indebted to the language of the church, while that of Michael was the formal *katharevousa*, the language of the law. They accepted their language as something given, a vehicle for expression with which one did not experiment.

But though they were Constantinopolitans by choice, they were also Chiots by ancestry, and this provided George Theotokas with the heritage of concern for the condition of the Greek language. By some historical coincidence, both Adamantios Korais and Jean Psycharis, the two major theoreticians of the language struggle in modern Greece (the former the proponent of the purist, the latter of the demotic) were also of Chiot ancestry. Korais (or Coray) was born in Smyrna of Chiot parents and spent most of his life in the West, particularly in Amsterdam and Paris. That his linguistic compromise, the *katharevousa*, has ceased to be used by literary men for three generations must not blind us to the fact that his influence was titanic at the time, not only for his work on language, but also for his editions of the classics and for his introductions to works that had a national as well as an educational objective. Jean Psycharis, another "Parisian Chiot" and professor of Oriental Languages at the Sorbonne, became the leading proponent of the demotic language and waged an unrelenting battle against the purists. His book *My Voyage*, published in 1888, created a stir in Greek circles and was—among other manifestations, including Palamas's poetry—a major contribution to the final victory of demotic Greek as a language of literature and, generally, of culture.

The interest of Theotokas in language was abiding; he broadened the position that the demotic tongue was the "national" speech of the Greek people by insisting that the language issue went beyond literature and impinged upon the political sphere. As he saw it, the victory of Demoticism was a guarantee that rational and democratic forces in other aspects of Greek life would eventually triumph, and Theotokas did everything he could—including writing well—to promote this victory. It is a tribute to his literary style that on reading his works, whether discursive or creative, one can briefly forget that the problem of language is a vexing one in Greek literature.

I Free Spirit

The young Theotokas was born and grew up, therefore, "in the shadow of the Patriarchate" (to use a favorite phrase of his), in a Constantinople that all Greeks had believed for centuries would once again be the center of the Hellenic world, a city whose great architectural monuments were daily reminders of the Greek nation's previous grandeur and international importance.

It was the brutal awakening of the Asia Minor Disaster of 1922 that put an end to the belief in the *Megale Idea* ("Great Idea") of reconquest of Constantinople and the reestablishment of Hellenism as a major force in the Near East that compelled Theotokas, as well as the rest of his countrymen, to view the hopes, illusions, and reality of Greece with the clarity and candor that became a life style for him.

Though his imagination may have been stunned into quietude by the impact of the Asia Minor Disaster that had befallen Greece, Theotokas's intellect and need for action were not stifled. "It was a terrible experience for a seventeen year old boy," he was to say in his early manhood. "For me, the first psychological result was that for a period, my poetic and artistic feelings were snuffed out."[1] It would be from the perspective of Western Europe, where he had gone for "free" studies at the Sorbonne and the University of London, that, under the pseudonym, Orestes Digenis, he was to write *Free Spirit* (1929), the brilliant critique of Greece and Greek values that auspiciously initiated his career as a writer and served as the document through which the aspirations of the Generation of the Thirties would first be expressed. But he was an activist as well as a thinker: he had been suspended from the University of Athens in 1926 for a publication of the Students' Company (*Foititiki Syndrofia*) and would not have received his degree if the Minister of Education had not resigned under the pressure of lead articles in the *Elefthero Vima* and the protests of a number of intellectuals.

The hope for a greater Greece was lost, Theotokas believed, and *Free Spirit* was the document by which he hoped to formulate what was left for his nation and people who had suddenly and brutally lost the great expectations that had sustained them. The Great Idea had perished on the quays of Smyrna and with it the hopes for an "imperial" and glorious Greece. Coming a century after the struggle for Greek independence, the Asia Minor Disaster put a limit to the young nation's geographical development and its expectations for the status of a major power. But the fact that Greece would remain a small power was no reason, he felt, for the nation's cultural development to cease.

Europe, after the First World War, struggled to understand the changed conditions of the twentieth century. But perhaps because she was exhausted, perhaps because many of the young who reached manhood in the years between 1910–1920, "the sacrificed generation . . . who were thoughtful and talented," had died in Macedonia and Asia Minor, Greece was unable to cope with the twentieth century. Having been bled during a decade of wars, Theotokas suggested, she lacked the strength and resilience. "We left everything as it was and entered the twentieth century with our eyes closed" (pp. 102–103).

But did an intellectual tradition exist that might have helped the Greeks respond to the issues of the new century, with or without a lost war? According to Theotokas, the only idea that seemed to sustain the Greeks since their Revolution in 1821 seemed to be the Great Idea, and the only problem Greece had confronted before the First World War was the language problem. Even that, because of an inability to compromise, could not be solved. Furthermore, the teachers, those who could be expected to guide the young through the web of conflicting loyalties, were unable to help. "Having devoted their lives to the study of ancient grammar, Roman law, Byzantine history, and the demotic song," that is, being narrow specialists and not men of scope and breadth, he wrote in *Free Spirit*, "they could not grapple with the rapid change of morals, the radical political and economic confusions, the class struggle, jazz and the world of passions it expressed, the restlessness of the postwar generation, modern girls with short-cropped hair and skirts above the knees. . ." (p. 101).

What seemed to be the problem with Greece, Theotokas asked. The fact that he had just turned twenty-three when he published his opinions in *Free Spirit* did not intimidate him from formulating an answer, for he had considered Greece with an open mind from an "airplane's perspective" of Europe: a metaphor, certainly, but an apt one. Greece, he concluded, perhaps unjustly, offered "nothing" to the "agitation that is contemporary Europe" because of a number of factors, among which were "scholasticism" and the "partisan spirit," an outgrowth of the "basic provincialism" of the Greeks, which was not modified by the continuation of their studies in German, Italian, French, or English universities. Instead of developing the European critical spirit, his compatriots accepted everything they were taught with undiscerning enthusiasm. He continues: "We have Germanized, Gallicized, Anglicized intellectuals [and] Moscovites, just as we have native intellectuals who are devoted to our narrow local traditions—ancestor-worship, the Byzantine past, and the demotic song—but we do not have real *Europeans*"(p. 13).

An obvious power was lacking in Greek intellectual life, certainly, but people who could listen to what others were saying were also difficult to find. There was no dialogue. Theotokas uttered this melancholy statement throughout his life: "Many people teach in Greece, from official and unofficial positions, from balconies, sidewalks, from every place." Despite the confidence of the "teachers" that what they said was gospel truth and the heavily footnoted books they wrote, the Greeks made no progress because what was really lacking were the "natural presuppositions of intellectual development . . . free thought, broad perspectives, the wealth and greatness of feeling" (pp. 17–18).

He pursued this theme in an essay entitled "National Character and Intellectual Militarism," in which he attempted to break away from the glib formulas that so many contemporary Greek writers evidently found attractive. Before "Demoticism" (a movement that not only won a place in Greek cultural life for the demotic speech but also attempted to discover what was unique about modern Greece), the intellectuals were "ancestor-worshippers." Later, with men like Ion Dragoumis, but particularly with Fotos Politis and Yiannis Apostolakis, there was the cry to return to the folk and Byzantine traditions and to the works of Solomos and Papadiamandis as foundations for the new litera-

ture that would be written. This was the "formula." The Greek
artist, according to the way Theotokas read Politis, should express his "ego-character and his environment"; but this, Theotokas cautioned, would tend to limit his "external world to the
boundaries of his [own] land" (p. 24).

Why should the "Greek self" be limited by the schema of a
passing dogmatist? "Traditions" of this sort were just a new
kind of *katharevousianism,* he claimed, limiting the freedom of
the artist by trying to set up a Procrustean bed on which he
would be measured to see how "national" he could be considered. It was not only the purists, therefore, but demoticists
like Fotos Politis as well who ignored and attacked the present
and looked to the past for guidance on how to behave and how
to create. Greek art, the demoticists said, must be "Greek," an
art that demanded the creator work not only for the "national
good" but in "total awareness of its national purpose" (p. 42).

Nationalists like Fotos Politis, Theotokas claimed, were no
different from the Marxists; both were narrow-minded dogma-
tists who distorted things in order to fit them into their formulas,
intellectual militarists who feared the daemon and wanted to
fetter the "free spirit." The young must break with the past,
must surpass the traditional and secure. The fetters that bound
them were the dogmas of which Greeks seemed to be so fond.
Only the "free spirit" could create art, he maintained; for this
reason it is difficult to impose "national" or "social" goals on
a poet. Theotokas viewed these demands as attempts by the
older generation to impose its values on the young, to manipu-
late them into becoming executors of the values they themselves were unable to establish.

The days of the heroic poets and conquistadors like Ion
Dragoumis, Lorenzo Mavilis, and Pavlos Melas were over, "older
and wiser people say." What were needed now were polite,
hardworking, positive scientists and engineers, not dreamers.
But, Theotokas countered, the streets of Athens and of the entire
land were full of "good youths," and because of them Greece
had not created anything beautiful or great. "We," he says,
"want inflamed spirits ... unbowed, dissatisfied adventurers of
the spirit and the mind, people impelled beyond the horizons
and above the level of the herd by the abundance of forces

within them. These 'prodigal sons' maintain the flame." If they are missing, "your country—no matter how much you may tidy it up—will not be worth much" (p. 57). Woe be to Greece if she bases her future on the "well-behaved lads," because she will be a tamed land, a Mediterranean Switzerland. "Is this possible for the land of Odysseus?"

How will the "free spirit" affect literature, which is the means by which a people speak to and understand themselves? A quick glance backward to the past century revealed to Theotokas that Greece had been a "receiving" nation intellectually, taking influence from all of Europe but giving none. Doubtless, the greatest literary expression had been lyric poetry, but even then "no girl from a foreign country has had her restlessness, her dreams, her unhappiness reflected in the lines of Solomos, Mavilis, Palamas, or Gryparis" (p. 50).

The situation was one to cause despair when one considered the atrophied condition of Greek prose. Theotokas was not the first to point this out. Jean Psycharis said much the same thing in 1903: "The critical time for a nation is the hour when it begins to write in prose,"[2] for only then can its language be considered mature enough for the critical discourse so necessary to carry on the everyday business of its civilization with reason and efficiency.

Prose is the tool of man firmly fixed in his family, his class, his society, his historical epoch. If poetry is the individual voice speaking the profoundest truths about man as a being, prose— and particularly fiction—is the spider's web of factual reality in whose filaments the individual is fixed, and even trapped, by the minutiae of his specific existence. Poetry does not require a society. On the contrary, prose is the *vehicle* of society. Perhaps not only the vehicle but the gauge as well, for the social novel, to give one example, cannot exist in a rural nation without urban centers large enough to maintain a number of social classes interacting with one another. It would be difficult to challenge this observation without offering examples of writers who produced novels of society within a nonurbanized nation.

Before the Asia Minor Disaster the Greek writers, in Theotokas's opinion, were "feeble compared to the poets ... mere entertainers." Those writers of prose who had the greatest influence had been men like Roidis, Psycharis, and Dragoumis, not in their creative but in their critical work. Instead of the social novel, Greek writers had concentrated on *ethographia,* descriptions of customs and characters in the Greek countryside or the slowly growing urban centers, rarely if ever producing a large-scale architectural work. According to Theotokas, ethography was a limited genre that may have provided descriptions of lovely regions, interesting customs, and quaint characters, but it could not provide the thrust of powerful themes, well-defined conflicts, and major characters. In lacking creative powers, these works lacked all. "They leave no impression on us," he said. "We forget them immediately." The ethographers, since they viewed men as types, considered their duty complete when their characters had fulfilled themselves as types. The academic writers did likewise, except more theoretically, while the Marxists went even further by defining their characters within social and economic classes.

If a writer wanted to prove a point, Theotokas maintained, he should avoid fiction and write essays or propaganda leaflets. In its own right, discursive writing is important to a culture and helps enrich the writers themselves. But in Greece, "land of half-learning," this "scholarly fiction" was a burden to creative literature. Art is not a logical construct but spirit, and a work lacks everything if it lacks spirit.

No writer, he continued, had so far breathed life into any of his characters. Thus, Greek fiction lacked not only great characters like Emma Bovary, Anna Karenina, or Julien Sorel, but also humble and real people.[3] After a hundred years of political freedom and half as much of literary ethography, Greek literature could be characterized as anemic. Its weakness was internal because it lacked powerful thought and inspiration. To live a *full* life, he repeated the Psycharis dictum, Greece must have the essence, which was prose! The Greeks can no longer live on poetry, or ethography, on dogmatic pronouncements, or on the speeches of political candidates. The older writers may have been satisfied to write about the mountain communities, the fishing villages, and the city neighborhoods with their taverns and coffeehouses, but this new generation, he proclaimed, has greater demands placed on it.

The new generation had Europe and the twentieth century to contend with and they must now do so as equals. To do this they must reject the systems and formulas presented to them by those who wanted to limit this freedom of action and of thought. The intellectuals of the new generation must reject the easy dogmatisms of the past, the "truth-seeming interpretations of the world and of humanity." They must, on the contrary, "plunge into the unseen worlds that hide beneath the visible reality" and must be "frightened by the weakness of [their] thought." They must not be "satisfied by systems presented ready made," nor believe in generalizations not founded on reality as they can observe it. These abstractions cannot fit the inexhaustible richness of reality. The new generation must "understand something—something that is *its own*."[4]

This had happened before in modern Greek history, Theotokas reminded his readers—once with the Revolution and again when men of the Generation of the 1880s like Palamas and Psycharis overturned the "middle ages." Things can change when a spirited people like the Greeks have reached the final depths of despair, when a group breaks with the "diseased past and forges ahead. They seize their ungoverned powers, imbue them with their own awareness, and urge them toward new directions. They begin a new epoch" (p. 105).

Brave words, and many of them true. They have the intense confidence of youth in its own opinion and much of its blindness. But partial blindness is often necessary to the young; otherwise, they would tend to compromise too early. Theotokas, in *Free Spirit*, was unable to see the greatness of Alexander Papadiamandis, but the powerful writer from Skiathos totally ignored the groundswell of Demoticism and wrote in a mixture of contemporary newspaper style and of personal diction. To have accepted the possibility that great literature can be written in a sterile language might have jeopardized the Greek writer's first order of business, which was agreement on the language of the people as a vehicle for their expression. Very much like Seferis, the young Theotokas was unable to see the greatness of Cavafy, not because of the mixed language and indifference to Demoticism of the Alexandrian poet, but because his work was the supreme example of the tendency of a certain school of

Greek poetry to write about despair and the themes of defeat and death. Whoever considered Cavafy an avant-garde poet, Theotokas believed, distorted both the Alexandrian's work and the meaning of avant-garde. "Mr. Cavafy is an end and avant-garde poetry is a beginning," he stated. "The only influence Mr. Cavafy can exercise on a young, living generation is a negative one. In expediting the end of one epoch of Greek letters, he may help another to emerge" (p. 108). For this same reason, both Theotokas and Seferis were cool in their youth to the verse of Constantine Karyotakis.

The new generation, soon to be called "the Generation of the Thirties," must be imbued, Theotokas believed, with the necessity for consolidating the victory of Demoticism and for confronting the problems of Greece with dedication and confidence. There must be no place for retreat in the language struggle or for a failure of nerve. The postwar era beckoned and there was much for Theotokas and his contemporaries to do. There would be time to rehabilitate Papadiamandis and Cavafy. Theotokas himself would grapple with their significance when the first achievements of his generation allowed him to believe that the objectives he had outlined in *Free Spirit* would eventually be attained. But in 1929, on the threshold of the new decade and of their careers, the young people of a post-Disaster Greece would be better off to reject the crutches of the past and to learn to walk upright toward the glowing era that Theotokas felt certain was about to dawn.

Despite the few errors of judgment present in this youthful work, *Free Spirit* remains one of the significant landmarks in the achievement of the Generation of the Thirties. Later on, Theotokas would correct the relatively minor lapses that were inescapable results of his spirited call for something new. Besides, compared to the scores of manifestos written at the time, *Free Spirit* holds up rather well after virtually half a century. This slender book is a crucial document for the study of the literature that was to be written by the men and women who had attained majority after the Asia Minor Disaster of 1922, because it clarified the issues they faced and articulated their demands for a literature that would be experimental as well as responsive to the social realities.

Because of Theotokas, the group of young writers known as the Generation of the Thirties achieved "the first sign of their self-knowledge," writes Constantine Dimaras. After the publication of *Free Spirit*, and as a result of the literary production of the other writers, there was to be a "differentiation of idiosyncracies" in the opinion of this historian of modern Greek literature and himself a member of the same generation, but *Free Spirit* remains a "sure guide for whoever desires to be introduced to the historical issues of the generation for which George Theotokas is one of the most characteristic representatives."[5]

II   *The Young Ideologue*

Who belonged to the Generation of the Thirties and where did this group of writers first manifest itself? Theotokas gives us a clue for the latter: it was in the Students' Company (formed in 1909), an undergraduate version of the Educational Association.[6] Both organizations were outgrowths of the demotic movement armed for conflict with established conservative forces in Greek life. If to these two we add a third, the *Noumas* (founded in 1903), the first combative periodical of Demoticism, we see that all three manifestations were based on the great importance of language. It was through the Students' Company, a blend of discussion and political action group that would eventually be Theotokas's model for the "Argo" section of his first novel, that the young intellectuals of the Generation of the Thirties met each other.

The last voyage of Psycharis to Greece in the summer of 1925, among other things to choose a gravesite in Chios, was the occasion of a series of programs given in his honor by the Students' Company. Theotokas later mourned the fact that he and his friends had not published the speeches they gave in the linguist's honor, explaining that "one day we must agree to write the Company's history ... [because] its importance increases with the passage of time. ... The initial purpose of the Students' Company was to represent and pass on the spirit of Demoticism within the university." According to Theotokas, it took on a more general character spontaneously, providing a forum for the intellectual students and becoming "the center that molded and expressed the restlessness, the quests, the awareness of the new generation—that generation that was later to be called 'of the Thirties' and that was, in actual fact, the first Greek generation of the twentieth century."[7]

The students lionized Psycharis but were surprised by his conservative ideas. "He was a man of the Great Idea," Theotokas recalled in *Intellectual Journey*. "He spoke of the 'King Turned to Marble' and of the eternal dreams of the race with an impassioned voice and sparkling eyes" (p. 203). On November 20, 1925, at the hall of the Society for Social and Political Sciences, five students lectured on the Master: Ilias Tsirimokos discussed "Psycharis and the Students' Company"; Linos Politis treated "Psycharis and the Language Issue"; Yiannis Oikonomidis studied "Psycharis the Writer"; George Theotokas analyzed "The Social Significance of Psycharis"; and Constantine Th. Dimaras gave a talk entitled "In Praise of Psycharis."

They had discovered themselves as a group (others, no less talented, eventually would join them), and they knew their objectives.[8] All that remained was a periodical that they themselves could control and that would necessarily express their attitudes. The periodical was not to be founded for a few years. In the meantime, there was *Kyklos*, the journal of Apostolos Melachrinos, who made no claims that his journal had a specific artistic point of view. Theotokas contributed a number of his early efforts to the journal, but as it demanded only that writers "subject themselves to the demands of art and our newer form of language," it could by no stretch of the imagination be considered a vehicle for the young.

Idea, a monthly that lasted for fifteen issues, came closer to fulfilling that requirement. Founded and edited by Spyros Melas, Yiannis Oikonomidis, and Theotokas, it was to be "the organ of free thought and art." Melas (1882–1966), the chief-editor, was older of course, but the journal attempted at least initially to deal honestly with the issues by which the Generation of the Thirties was confronted. As its title indicates, *Idea* was a journal for a then suspect idealism. Its general principles were instructive. It was "designed to attack certain weaknesses—the lack of Greek self-confidence—and to support certain values for Greek youth." It would combat materialist "theories of causality" that robbed man of his free will. Since idealism had been harmed by capitalism, *Idea* would be the organ of the "free spirit," above parties and social classes and against demagoguery from every direction. Among other things, *Idea* would combat barren photographic realism, sometimes identified with ethography; class-oriented and propagandist art; "sick postwar inclinations that express every physical and spiritual pleasure"; and the spirit of blind modernity. Its final principle was to use a demotic language that was "national" and that did not insist on class distinctions or class politics.[9]

Except possibly for the puritanism of the third statement, the general principles seem fairly characteristic of Theotokas's ideas as they had been expressed in *Free Spirit*, although he tended at the time to be unnecessarily frightened by jazz and its spiritual implications.

The presence of Spyros Melas in the editorial trinity possibly explains the emphasis on "idealism"; his erratic behavior later on—particularly during the German Occupation—was probably symptomatic of his early position. The periodical ceased publication in 1934, but during its short life it was a platform for the combative center as it was swirled about by the Fascist right and the Communist left.

For a political and temperamental moderate, Theotokas surprises one with his inability to bypass literary squabbles. If he was the official combatant for *Idea*, he was certainly not a timid contributor to *Kyklos*, for quite early in the periodical's career Theotokas took on Aristos Kambanis, one of the important conservative critics of Greece, and a man who was later to achieve a powerful position in the dictatorship of Metaxas.

Kambanis, whom the twenty-five-year-old Theotokas considered a light, frivolous character lacking ideas of his own, became a target for an article, because "he pays me the honor of discussing me often." One day Kambanis will be important, Theotokas predicted, because he knows how to "respect true wisdom." How does he do this? By ridiculing quietly and subtly all those who try to do something without attempting to do anything himself, by pretending to be a man who could accomplish great things if he wished, by attacking all books but writing only short articles as a precaution against being attacked himself, by criticizing all new ideas but having none himself, and by enjoying the Attic sky without effort, struggle, or worries.[10]

"The Attic sky" is a deceptive phrase hiding within it a controversy that will emerge in the second half of the decade with the issue of "Greekness." Standing for clarity and precision, it was the symbol of those who, like Kambanis and his friend Pericles Yiannopoulos, demanded that Greek culture reflect its geography and natural surroundings, removed from foreign influences, which they considered noxious. "The Attic sky" imposed upon Greeks the harsh clarity of reason, while those whose thoughts were vague and unclear were presumably victims of ideas that could not withstand the pellucid Aegean light. Psycharis himself had diagnosed "a Greek disease" which Theotokas explained as "[our] national vagueness and [our] inability to apprehend matters in their clear and concentrated form, a bent toward the incoherent and murky, and, from there, toward confusion and anarchy."[11] This was directly attributable to the language problem, however, and its therapy demanded first that the disorder of the written language, which was the vehicle of education and the expression of culture, be set right before "we can impose order on our minds."

Language, tradition, culture, and nationality are concepts related in Theotokas's thinking, and the superficially linguistic conflict between the demoticists and the purists found its resonance deep in the racial psyche. The greatest mistake made during the language struggle, Theotokas believed, was that the form of the Greek language had become a political and ideological issue, had frozen thinking in both camps, and had caused havoc for more than half a century. That the problem has yet to be resolved may be, as Theotokas often maintained, an indication of the inability of the Greek to think pragmatically, preferring to lock himself into iron-clad dogmas. He once suggested that the issue of language be completely divorced from politics so that a "linguistic compromise, satisfying to all parties" could be reached. Otherwise, the vendetta between Right and Left would never terminate, and education and culture would not proceed without the constant interruptions that occur when governments change.[12]

His belief that the condition of the Greek language was directly responsible for the imprecision of much Greek thought was not as stoutly maintained at the beginning of his career as it was later on. In the early 1930s Theotokas believed, as did most of the other demoticists, that the triumph of the popular speech would occur in the near future and be absolutely definitive.

To convince his audience, therefore, Theotokas would not feel as though he were using an invalid argument if he employed a rhetorical technique that Aristos Kambanis would find congenial. Unweighted by chauvinism and totalitarianism, "the Attic sky" argument was one that Theotokas would find useful in trying to prove his case.

"Clarity of style is the light of intellect," he wrote in an essay published in *Kyklos* in 1931, "[and it] means primarily that the writer understands" what he himself is writing. The vagueness and inaccuracy of much Greek prose, he claimed, can be found in newspapers and periodicals, in speeches of politicians, even in the laws themselves. But what is clarity?

... Clarity is not a school lesson. It is a mold of nature, [and] fills the atmosphere we breathe. ... Greece is all spirit. It is a land of pure and clear thoughts. ... There is no place here for heavy and dark intellectual structures, for cloudy systems, for pompous and grandiloquent exaltations, for arrogant and gross hues. ... Everything here is simple, so beautifully, so profoundly simple that their simplicity has been called a *miracle*. ... For how long shall we continue to ignore the great lesson that our land offers us? For how long shall we undergo this barren submission to the blind instincts or the murky mysticisms and the perverse ways of thought of foreign and distant peoples who have never encountered the Greek light ... ?[13]

In the pages of *Idea,* Theotokas battled for the values of liberal democracy and individual and intellectual freedom against the two grinding wheels of what he termed the "Teutonic" teachers, Nietzsche and Marx. Both world theories fathered by these two men, Theotokas claimed in "Freedom and Force," demand and exalt discipline and narrow-mindedness, and both hate liberal freedom, which they consider a fruit of bourgeois civilization in a state of corruption. "Democracy is difficult," he continued, and it is simpler to reject this difficult way of life and to accept one in which the more powerful decide; simpler, possibly, but threatening to all human values, for as Theotokas reminds his readers, the Pangalos dictatorship, frequently cited for the absurd puritanism of trying to legislate the length of women's skirts, was also responsible for setting up a gallows in an Athenian square and decreeing capital punishment to be determined retroactively. In a footnote he stated that only the Students' Company objected to this formally in a general meeting on December 1, 1925. The rest of Athenian society was cowed. Freedom, he concluded, was more important even than the "most imperative interests of society and the state. The spirit first, man first, and everything else will follow."[14]

But the "intellectual militarisms" of Right and Left were not to be swayed by appeals to liberal democratic freedoms. Kambanis in *Neos Kosmos,* and Kostas Varnalis and Dimitris Glinos in *Anaghenisis* and *Rizospastis,* communist journals, attacked him and *Idea,* but Theotokas was not one to retreat from a squabble. In a devastating critique of Varnalis's "The Light That Sears," the first clearly political poem of Varnalis, Theotokas criticized it as unpoetic, barren, and pedestrian and attacked the poet for what he felt was heavy and unsophisticated propaganda, half-learning, courting of the mob, and hatred of those who disagreed with him. They had met once, Theotokas continued, and he had found Varnalis to be an "honorable, sincere and good man," but he considered his work imbued with a "lust for revenge." He ended by warning Varnalis that he might be forgotten by the proletarians as soon as they learned to read and write. "That would be the hardest punishment of the artists of Mr. Varnalis's group. The same proletarians, once they are civilized, will forget them and read the *others.* Plato, Pascal, Goethe. . . ."[15]

It is Glinos's turn next. In "A Disastrous Misstep," a polite, respectful but nevertheless strong attack on the change of course he detected in the leading political theoretician of the Left, Theotokas reprinted Glinos's ideas from the newsletter of the Students' Company (March 1, 1926) that Demoticism was a national and classless issue, and claimed that Glinos's veering toward the extreme Left resulted in the dissolution of the Educational Association and almost in the collapse of the movement of educational demoticism. As Theotokas said of Glinos in the late 1920s during the halcyon days of the Students' Company:

He was a *leftist*, certainly . . . with the meaning that we too are *leftists*; that is, he criticized the imbalance and injustice of capitalism and believed in the need of social progress beyond the bounds of the status quo toward a more just and peaceful society. But he also believed as we did in the superiority of intellectual values and the need for freedom and social peace.[16]

Theotokas himself believed in freedom of thought, certainly, for others as well as for himself. In the spring of 1932, he and a group of writers (including Galateia Kazantzakis, Kostas Ouranis, and Constantine Dimaras) formed a *Pen* club in Athens and took part in a conference of the International *Pen* club in Ragusa, Dalmatia, on May 25, 1933, where Hitler's Germany was condemned for persecuting intellectuals and burning books.[17] Before going to Dalmatia, Theotokas prepared the ground for his gesture by agreeing with the "theoreticians of the Left" that capitalism was bankrupt, but he rejected violent revolution in favor of democratic change. He would, he stated, be willing to see democracy proceed leftward even faster than he thought it was going as long as "freedom of the intellect and the free functioning of the government apparatus" could be guaranteed. *Idea* had been accused of being Fascist, but idealistic intellectuals "have everywhere attacked fascism. . . . If there exists a class in Germany that has reacted against tyranny, it is not the working class but the intellectuals who profess what 'we' profess. Everywhere, however, fascism finds warm followers in the ranks of the Marxists. And a few leaders. The enemies of freedom communicate well among themselves."[18]

His clearest and most philosophical position on the world theory he professed can be found in *Forward to the Social Problem* (1932) a pamphlet dedicated "to the young" and written to inform them about the problems of their time. It is a return to the exhortations of *Free Spirit* written three years later as the economic crisis and the political climate of Greece, always in a state of typhonic agitation, were making his centrist position difficult to maintain.

His generation, Theotokas maintained, had been educated in the "School of War" and had been imbued with a "malignant nationalism" that taught all the children of Europe to hate "like young wolves." Since their elders were unable to teach them anything through their simplistic textbooks, the young were condemned to be educated by the books that "reflected their distrust, their doubts, their negations, their thirst for new values." Despite the "Dadaisms and surrealisms . . . the worship of Negro Art, the repellent literary fashion of . . . sexual perversion" and the attack on the virtues of coherence and clarity in art, it was an exciting era in which to be young, and those who were able to pursue their studies in Europe were no less perplexed than those who were "educated" here, in the "upside-down Greece of the refugees, military coups, civil war, and intellectual chaos. . . ."[19]

The social problem to which he addressed himself, however, was the catastrophic effect of the worldwide economic crisis of 1929, which forced the bourgeois class for the first time to doubt the values it had always accepted. The Renaissance ideal, "the equilibrium of the needs of the mind, the heart, and the body" that grew out of the medieval orientation to God, was now losing ground to the materialism that had been introduced by machine civilization. Greece, made backward by the long Turkish occupation, was now placed in the intolerable position of being forced to choose between a Europe in decline and an expanding Russia.

Theotokas's attack on communism surprises the reader not only by its ferocity but by its relative precociousness. It is an antibolshevism that western intellectuals have been accustomed to writing and expressing, particularly after World War II; but out of what social climate did it arise in 1932? The diction is certainly not unusual coming from a Greek intellectual of the upper-middle class, but Theotokas seems to have anticipated the social conflicts that were to sear Greece almost two decades later, by which time he would have gone beyond them and called for coexistence.[20]

Theotokas attacked communism as a rigid, dogmatic system that would crush *"the freedom of the human spirit* that began in the Renaissance." He viewed historical materialism not as an objective science but as a subjective expression of a class that wanted to dominate society. He considered socialism, with which he identified himself, as an outgrowth of a European liberalism that began with the French Revolution and that, throughout history, had remained western and humanistic in orientation, cautious of "revolutionary adventures" that might crush the human spirit and put an end to freedom. Since he treasured dialogue and the "orderly conflict of ideas and of political and social movements," he pitted himself against the "materialistic mysticism" that was communism, that "strange mixture of Slavic and Asiatic fanaticism and German scientism," whose twin hopes were the machine and the mass.[21]

An enemy of communism, yet unable to defend capitalism, particularly when it was in abject disarray even in the United States, Theotokas posited another solution, one that would provide a more stable and just society, that would maintain the Western traditions with which he allied himself, and that would solve the crisis communism claimed it could solve by means that he rejected.

Believing that social classes and nations would never be eradicated and sensing that laissez-faire capitalism had been permanently destroyed by the Depression, he advocated a tentative version of a European Common Market in which the "industrial means of production" would be government-controlled and in which socialization would be controlled by an "international economic discipline."[22]

This ideal political entity, a European Economic Community two decades before its time, would appear to satisfy all the economic and social interest groups, though how this could be achieved without force, or without a Second World War, Theotokas did not say, assuming perhaps too generously that the privileged classes would retreat and that the nations with political, historical, and geographical demands would allow their grievances to be decided by a perpetual arbitration board. Possibly Theotokas, as a friend of what he called the "Anglo-American civilization," hoped that Greece, and Europe, would follow the lead of the pragmatic "Anglo-Saxons," who could usually be counted on to compromise before an open break.

He accepted the concept of a directed economy, therefore, and even doubted that parliamentary government as Europe knew it was still workable. "Often Parliament is nothing more than a chance gathering of unqualified party bosses and hacks who represent nothing but local, party, and individual petty-interests."[23] But parliamentary democracy, though it may no longer represent the needs of contemporary society, was not to be rejected out of hand. Its values were worth defending, particularly since it had guaranteed freedom of thought, had lessened the possibilities of civil strife, and had limited the dangers of the extremes, "the inflamed minds of Right and Left."

He called on Europe to surpass the contemporary problems that plagued her with a new humanism that she will discover once again in "the School of Greece," from which "the hysterical prophets of our time have alienated her" and should attempt once more "to find herself in logic, in measure, in harmony, in intellectual and moral order, in the *health of the spirit.*" Europe, he maintained, would find this lost sense of equilibrium in neo-Hellenism; that is, in modern Greek civilization, which had not "yet achieved a clear sense of self" but which was "closer than any other nation to the traditions of the Greek spirit [and] has retained them instinctively and unconsciously." Because of this compelling need, the modern Greeks will be called upon, finally, "to speak their minds" (p. 59).

But which Greece, one might ask, would be called upon to lead Europe out of its spiritual quagmire? The "upside-down Greece of the refugees, military coups, civil war, and intellectual chaos"? Still the patriot, Theotokas was quite capable of being unmercifully critical of his homeland, but immediately he fell into the same "Attic sky" rhetoric he had condemned in others. Laissez-faire capitalism must go, but he had no illusions that when it disappeared man would be without blemish:

The mass will always be incoherent, will-less and senseless, and it will know this and will call on its superiors to govern it. And luckily, superior men, with spirit or will or with both will always exist. These will compose always a *natural and unavoidable and eternal oligarchy.* (p. 51)

Three years later he was to witness the coup of Colonel Kondylis, who returned the monarchy, and the following year, 1936, the military takeover of General Metaxas, who was appointed by the newly installed King George. Were these the "superior men" Theotokas was confident would always lead

the "incoherent, will-less and senseless mass" and perpetually
"compose the natural and unavoidable and eternal oligarchy"?
Or were they merely the expressions of the oligarchy Theotokas
was himself to battle against later in his life when he thought
internal strife had been surpassed in Greece?

How ironic all this sounds when one considers Theotokas
just before his death, the stalwart fighter for parliamentary
democracy, the Olympian figure in the "upside-down Greece . . .
of military coups" who descended from the apolitical stance
he had assumed immediately after the Second World War and
began to battle the forces in Greece that, with King Constantine's
removal of the Prime Minister, initiated the long descent to
the military coup that George Theotokas warned the Greeks was
coming but that he did not live to see.

CHAPTER 2

Early Fulfillment

I Leisure Hours

THEOTOKAS had published a number of fictional pieces in *Kyklos* that showed, if not an original creative talent, at least a fresh attitude toward literature. His major work, *Argo,* a novel many of his friends knew he was writing, was still a few years off in 1931, when he published *Leisure Hours,*[1] a collection of four "psychographic sketches," part discursive interior monologue and dialogue, part fiction. In no other work is Theotokas so successful in maintaining a vagrant, fugitive mood and a playful sense of humor. It is a young man's book, confident and fresh, full of the twenty-five year old's confusions, vitality, and loneliness; his concern about the future of Greece counterbalanced by his desire for sexual conquest; his awareness of time's passing and of the inevitability of death.

The first sketch, "Contraditions of Loneliness," a monologue employing the principles of free association rather than of logical order, is an *étude* on the difficulty of communication. Theotokas, the young, bachelor lawyer, leaves the divorce court on a lovely evening and walks through a twilight Athens. The issue of legal "incompatibility" occupies his mind initially, but he is soon in deeper water: how can society expect two people to agree when, on many issues, a person cannot maintain a consistency of thought with himself? Each human being has a simplified face he wears in public to mask the great complexity he bares in his moments of privacy. The real face remains silent while the "mask" talks incessantly. Men are basically lonely and complex, life is short, and it is difficult to sound the depths of one's soul.

In "Letter to a Provincial Girl," we have another sketch on a similar theme, except that the friend, Phrosini, reminds him

39

of his deepest self, someone who loves freely, not caring whether she scandalizes the neighbors, whose middle-class fears and puritanical respectability might act as a brake on the less confident. She is a free spirit, an islander like those whom Theotokas characterizes as pirates and corsairs: "I believe with all my heart in the values of our piratical traditions. Such a crazy people will never be lost even though the world is destroyed." As long as dreams exist on the shores of Greece, "we fear no one." But the islanders who emigrated because Greece was too small for them, who grew rich in foreign lands, did so for material things.

> ... When are we going at last to start that other adventure, the most fascinating and mad one, toward the intellectual unknown? When are we going to see the great free corsairs of the spirit, the unbound and legendary conquerors of the immaterial world, launch themselves from our shores again? (p. 67)

Why can't the Greek intellectuals, he asks, dare as much in their realm, that of the mind and spirit, as their more humble compatriots, the immigrants who built churches and schools for the communities they founded all over the world, dared do in the realm of matter?

"Lady on a Train" is a fine, humorous piece about a young man, going off to studies in Paris and London—cities he is certain were being built for ten centuries for him alone—and meeting a woman on the train whose loneliness, or aloneness, acts as a goad and a challenge to his masculinity. The conversation they exchange is dull indeed compared to the dialogue that sparkles in his mind, which is feverish with desire for her. In his fantasy he is constantly possessing her, though it is otherwise in drab reality.

Ideas exist in this highly successful sketch, but they are subordinated to scene, mood, and character. "The Goddess," the sketch that follows, is comparatively weak because the woman is a symbol of "art," and the desire the young man feels for her is a spiritual one. The reader is informed, of course, but certainly not charmed, as he was with "Lady on a Train." Yet both are important, the former because we see that Theotokas could break out of his studiousness into effervescent humor, while the latter brings him back to a profound seriousness about the destiny of Greece and the Greek people: "Your life, you think, is a wasted life, your century is an absurd century, your nation is a finished nation, dead and buried. Nothing good can come out of Greece, the black waves roar and echo within you, nothing good, nothing good..." (pp. 114–15).

II Argo

Theotokas had been working on a major novel for four years, but as *The Logbook of Argo and The Daemon* (1939) shows, he had been planning it for at least seven years, from as far back as 1928 in London. Its initial conception was not rational. He objected to forcing life, which is contradictory and unexpected, into a jail of form, with a "beginning, middle, and end." He changed his mind while writing *Argo*, however, and his logbook entry for November 1, 1935, states that "the way it is now being printed, in one volume, rather balanced, *with a beginning and an end,* seems sturdier to me" (italics mine).[2]

Argo aroused much controversy in Greek literary circles and, other than the full-length plays *Alcibiades* and *The Game of Folly vs. Virtue,* was to be the only major effort to represent Theotokas in translation. Book One, entitled "The Beginning," was published in the autumn of 1933 in a separate volume, containing the prologue, "A University Dynasty," about the Notaras family, the main body of the section, and concluding with "The Remarks of Lambros Christides." At first, Theotokas thought *Argo* should consist of three parts, but the initial plan was later changed somewhat, and the entire book was published in its final form in 1936, several months before the military coup by John Metaxas, whose censorship compelled Theotokas to publish the second edition in 1939 with the date of the first edition to avoid passing it through the censors.[3]

A bulky, untidy novel of 478 pages, which Theotokas was planning to make the beginning of a *roman fleuve, Argo* contains two plot lines that occasionally intersect and tells the story of the new generation of Greece after the Asia Minor Disaster.

The first story line involves the Notaras family, a great dynasty of professors of law at the University of Athens. Theofilos, the third Notaras, is the father of three of the major characters in *Argo*, Nikiforos, Alexis, and Linos. Sophia, the mother of the boys, feeling crushed in the loveless household of the cold professor, goes off to London and a life of hardship with an itinerant piano player, abandoning her sons to Aunt Lucia, a timid woman who lives a withdrawn, book-nurtured life.

Theofilos's idealism and absolutism, developed in Germany, "which he considered his second country,"[4] certainly influenced his thinking. Theotokas describes him as a man who would travel to "the end of the road," in other words, a man who pursues an idea to its ultimate conclusion "without fearing, without troubling himself about whether he was harming his own interests or the comforts of his life."

> ... Born with a peculiarity of this sort, it was natural that he would not experience intellectual doubts. From the first moment he began to think, he proudly accepted tradition without discussion. National ideals, the church, the glorious ancestors, the family, all these were for him sacred concepts that no one had the right to question.... Without these neither civilization nor humanity would exist, only the chaos of anarchy and bestiality. Because of this, whoever dared deny them was unbalanced, hysterical, epileptic, mad, unable to raise himself above the vulgarity of the instincts, to discipline his bodily passions, and to think logically. (pp. 18–19)

Notaras, because of the strength (or the rigidity) of his character, is a man who in times of historical and ideological chaos can command silence and respect from "the least disciplined audience in Greece," the students of the law school.

> ... The wars had ended, the Disaster had abruptly and rudely closed the first century of modern Greek independence. The second century was beginning in anarchy and discontinuity. Greece suddenly found herself without a form of government, without a constitution, without institutions or state organization, without ideologies, because all had been bankrupted in the conscience of the nation. (p. 40)

Nikiforos, the eldest, has been groomed to assume his father's position and to be the fourth Notaras of the dynasty, but living for a time in Germany, he is convinced that law is not his field. He abandons his studies, leads the artist's life in Paris, and returns to Athens where he publishes *The Purification*, a tragedy set in Constantinople at the time of the Fall. The play is quite successful: "The moderns applauded the untidiness and imbalance of *The Purification*. The conservatives could not acclaim such writing but neither could they condemn such flaming patriotism," (p. 36). Theofilos, who has not stopped supporting him, is surprised and proud of his son's success.

Since Nikiforos will not be the fourth member of the dynasty, the role presumably falls to Alexis, a shy, introspective boy who tries to suppress his poetic talents in order to be a Notaras, a cold, rational, willful man. He had "no confidence in his imagination and did not want to allow it to control his life. He feared its fickleness, its indefiniteness . . . and found in legal matters a hard but effective antidote for certain of his excessively romantic leanings, which he considered unhealthy" (p. 43).

Because Alexis's nature will not permit him to succeed his father at the university, the old man's hopes fall on Linos, the youngest and most handsome of the Notaras sons; but of all the sons Linos is most dominated by the vital forces, which slowly mature in him. His rebellion against books and education is the most serious revolt against the academic tradition of the Notaras family.

The Notaras are a family in decline, talented and interesting, but held together only by the youth of the sons. As soon as they grow old enough to lead their own lives, the centrifugal force of their differing personalities scatters them. They are like that other family in Theotokas's fiction, the ill-starred Christofis family in *The Daemon*,[5] which, unlike Thomas Mann's Buddenbrooks, who go from healthy dullness to feverish genius, reproduces its fever from generation to generation. Perhaps Theotokas wanted the Notaras to provide the reader with a sense of familial continuity in Greek public life, a measure by which to grant perspective to his two most successful characters, Pavlos Skinas and Damianos Frantzis. If this is so, the Notaras confuse more than they clarify. Frantzis and Skinas, on the contrary, have about them a truth and a definition that make them unmistakably Greek. Except for the end of their careers, when they cease to be convincing to the reader, Frantzis and Skinas are brilliant examples of certain Greeks as political animals.

Frantzis, with Alexis Notaras, is a member of "The Argo," a discussion group modeled on the Students' Company, "a circle of dissatisfied and unhappy students who wanted linguistic, educational, political, and even social reforms." They held lectures among themselves, heatedly discussed all the current theories, and published illegal periodicals and pamphlets. "Their membership contained royalists, nationalists, liberals, democrats, agrarians, social democrats . . ." and their heroes were as varied as Dostoevski, Solomos, Palamas, Cavafy, Valéry, Andre Gide, Bernard Shaw, Pirandello, and Rilke. For all their confusion, however, they were animated by similar concerns: ". . . the tragic fate of the Greek race, the weight of the great name, the idea of the insignificance of Greece in the contemporary intellectual life of the world." In their ideas these Argonauts were animated by "the Golden Fleece, the awakening of the Greek spirit; creation, Renaissance, glory. . . ."[6]

Like Greeks, however, they disagree more than they agree. The main issue at stake when the novel opens is a religious one. A communist speaker has offended the religious sensibilities of the Christians in "The Argo" and will not retract his statement. The Rightists in the group demand a recantation; when it is not forthcoming, they demand a vote on God's existence, which is decided in the negative.

As a Communist, Frantzis is hostile to religion, but his background, rendered by Theotokas in a long and masterful narrative, clearly the best section in the book (pp. 128–84), exhibits him as a man who needs a dogmatic religion to believe in. When Orthodox Christianity proves inadequate for him, he accepts Marxist communism with the dedication of a Byzantine.

Damianos Frantzis is an impressive portrait of a committed political man whose ruthless idealism serves as a balance to the career of Pavlos Skinas. The student allows Theotokas to express the Marxist view of history, both world and Greek, from the perspective of a social democrat, while Skinas, the politician on the ambitious climb to success, is characterized as a renegade socialist who loses interest in the social struggle once he learns how to attain personal success. These two are responsible for whatever dramatized ideas are to be found in the book, and their clash might have made *Argo* a great European novel had it not been muffled by the padding of the other characters who got in the way.

We follow Frantzis in his short, eventful life from the teeming proletarian quarter of Constantinople to the Athens slums of the Asia Minor refugees after the Disaster. Left to his family, young Damianos would have been uneducated, living submerged far below the level where ideas have any relevance. But his uncle, Isidoros Frantzis, priest at the Panaghia of Galata, sees his fierce desire for learning and enrolls him in the public school of the Greek community at Galata, where a "young Macedonian teacher named Pavlos Skinas taught." There is about Skinas that same fresh idealism that the still-undeveloped Franzis will later express, but he is less grounded in dogma and more inclined to personal glory and improvisation. "He dreamed of becoming leader of Hellenism and conquering the city" (p. 137), and the reader understands that Theotokas wants to create with Skinas a composite of Pavlos Melas and Ion Dragoumis, the former a hero of Macedonia and the latter a theoretician of the Great Idea in its later stages, who acted as an agent for the Greeks in his role as consul to the Porte. Skinas, too, is an operative, and he is forced to flee, hiding from the Turkish authorities briefly in Papasideros's church. Before his exposure, as a favor to the priest who befriends him and recounts the traditional stories of the Fall, Skinas takes an interest in Damianos, helping him somewhat, but this is soon ended when he is compelled to flee the city.

The young Frantzis, awakened to ideas and the thrill of education, is unwilling to submit to his father's cruel and short-sighted demands that he go to work. "I want to learn, I want to learn!" he shouts, and when compelled to labor all day, the young boy decides to leave home. Like his teacher, he goes to Papasideros's church, expecting sanctuary. The priest, therefore, protects both his nephew and Skinas and, imbuing them with the traditional stories of Greek suffering and aspirations, becomes a father figure to both. In a way, Skinas and Frantzis are thus "brothers," and the church of the Panaghia of Galata is their analogue to the Notaras mansion in Athens: both are swept away by history, the former in one titanic event, and the latter in a series of developments that undermine its specious stability.

After that brief meeting, teacher and pupil go their own way. Damianos goes to the theological school at Halkis, where his brilliance impresses everyone, but he cannot convince anyone that his religious vocation is genuine. The lonely boy loves the religious life, but his attitude to Christianity is complicated and perhaps marred by his inability to distinguish between Orthodoxy and Hellenism, a failing Theotokas pointed out more than once as an intellectual characteristic of the Greek. There is much of the Great Idea intermingled in Damianos's religion, and when the disastrous awakening occurs in 1922 and the Great Idea perishes on the quays of Smyrna, his religion is jettisoned as well.

Aghia Sophia was still Moslem. The bright plans of 1918 were optical illusions, hallucinations, dreams. The return to reality was, in truth, very painful. It had not come, then, the fulfillment of time, the historical moment, the hour of the Great Idea, which everyone awaited with such faith and longing for five tormented and tear-stained centuries. It was all lies! (p. 154)

He leaves the theological school for Athens and law studies, slowly breaking away from "all the traditions of the race, the wreck of the Great Idea, the Marbled King, the Doomed City" (p. 164) until he confronts a void that he must somehow fill. He has lived a life of illusion. Religion for him had been a means of keeping alive the national identity, but "without these national passions Orthodoxy lost its meaning and purpose." Christ was no longer the "warrior God" or even the "sweet and consoling god, as he was termed by the other peoples," but a "defeated general, with broken sword, who followed his army in despair on the road of retreat" (p. 166). Not only national and intellectual bankruptcy, but the uprooting from his environment alienated Damianos totally from his past. In Athens, he wakes up to social problems by seeing the differences between the rich and the poor.

Thinkers like Theofilos Notaras are unable to inspire him with their dry legalisms and their cold logic. Damianos chances upon a "red pamphlet," *The Communist Manifesto,* and sees the world fall into place. "For every question there was now an answer . . ." (p. 174). He was led to "the Promised Land . . . [of] superhuman Happiness. . . ."

And for this great Salvation it was worth sacrificing all the little freedoms, worth this great Happiness that the thousand-times dismembered peoples be torn apart once more and worse than ever, worth the great Atonement that rivers of blood be shed by the sinful race. It was worth it that all the works of genius and labor throughout the ages be destroyed so that—at long last—the ultimate structure for Humanity be built. (p. 175)

It is as a member of the Communist party that Damianos Frantzis meets Skinas again. The former teacher is now Minister of the Interior and has called the young Marxist into his office, having seen his name on a list of radical university students compiled by the police. Skinas offers him hopes, not very precise, which are predicated on his becoming an informer on his colleagues. This Frantzis immediately rejects.

Skinas, too, has his moral adventures: Frantzis manages to substitute one religion for another, whereas the Minister, as befits the traditional picture of the Greek politician, is guided only by what is in his own interest. Theotokas describes him as an outright careerist, reserving for him a cool sarcasm he seldom uses on any other major character. After a German education, he returns to Greece with his "a priori beliefs in Marxism, in historical materialism, and in socialism generally." But since Greece was a "backward, agrarian, and petit-bourgeois" country, the "natural prerequisites for socialism were lacking." In order that they exist "it was necessary that our society be organized on serious capitalistic bases" until Greece had attained her fair share of "proletarians and economic troubles," whereupon Skinas and his friends "would declare the class conflict" (p. 72). In order to develop the prerequisites for socialism, however, Skinas "entered by necessity the capitalistic environment, tasted the sweets of capitalism, became accustomed to them, and after a while had no desire at all to change things" (p. 73).

Skinas "had crept into a number of enterprises, initially as a middleman and later as a capitalist, managed great concerns, took sure risks. He was a Minister often. He fell, rose, changed party the way another changed shirts." But Theotokas holds back from the final insult to Skinas, for whatever could be said about him, "though he betrayed at times all ideas, all establishments, all parties, his friends, his women...I must say that he never betrayed the interests of the State" (p. 76).

By far Theotokas's most interesting characters in *Argo*, Frantzis and Skinas are the major actors in the novel's events. They are public men, whose interests draw the reader into the maelstrom of Greek life in the early thirties, while the Notaras sons, whether introspective or daemon-ridden, hesitant or decisive, drift through their era, more concerned with their personal development and pleasure than with what is occurring to their environment.

Book One (and, alas, *Argo* itself) reaches its climactic moments in a splendidly described attempted coup by a gang known as "The Military League" led by a General Tsaveas, a sort of man the fecund Greek army always seems to produce in great abundance, whose goal is "the salvation of the nation by any means" (p. 248). It is an open secret that the Military League will try to form a dictatorship, but when Skinas pleads with Armodios Zouganelis, the weak Prime Minister, an "ideal shop-keeper of the middle-class," to move against the plotters, he fails. Zouganelis, though far from a metaphysician, believes in "the will of the people," which its leaders must follow or be destroyed, as he claims the Greek people destroyed Harilaos Trikoupis and Venizelos. Tsaveas, on the contrary, believes in great men, "in History, in historical necessity, in historical laws," and has a head full of confused ideas to support his beliefs. "He had a deep contempt for politicians, newspapers and women..." and at this historical moment believes that his "mission was to upset Mr. Zouganelis and take his place and to cane the backsides of the journalists of all colors" (p. 250).

The great moment of Pavlos Skinas has come. Everything Theotokas has told the reader should lead him to believe that he will seize the moment with joy. He hesitates briefly between defending the government and assuming powers to which he has no legal right in order to move against the military. Skinas, as we know, has developed, if flexible, ideas and great ambition; the opportunity he has always wanted and needed appears, yet he must bide his time as the others in political authority are intimidated by the threat. General Ghialarakis, a Venizelist Cretan, appears and is willing to fight Tsaveas and "spill blood," but he needs a legitimate command from those in authority, who waver and fail to give the command. It would not be the first or the last time that Greek democrats would weaken when it came time to defend their form of government before outright military intervention.

When Skinas sees that no one is willing to command Ghialarakis to fight the units of Tsaveas, he "assumes the initiative and the responsibility." The legitimate government defeats the rebels, but when the battles are over the Greek people realize that Skinas is now in charge. Crowds, furious at the military intervention in the nation's political affairs, rush through Constitution and Omonia Squares. A group of Communist students battles a unit of marines; their leader, Damianos Frantzis, shoots and kills an officer; and the marines fire into the group and kill Linos Notaras and Dimitrios Mathiopoulos, a student recently converted from nationalism to communism. After a few pitched battles in which about fifty are killed, Pavlos Skinas speaks to the Athenians from a ministry balcony about sacrifices to which they must submit for the achievements he promises them.

Book One ends on a moment of high tension. Sandwiched between it and Book Two is "Intermedio," notes from a journal kept by a minor character, Lambros Christides, with a number of what might be labeled "impressive thoughts." The problem with the ineffectual Christides is that he is not essential to the novel. Perhaps Theotokas thought he needed him in order to enlarge his canvas of characters. His ideas, however, are not particularly exciting; one can almost call them pale. They suggest that Theotokas lost interest in *Argo* after Book One.

Book Two, consequently, reveals a decline in narrative interest, not only because the major emphasis of the action falls on the Notaras sons, but because Pavlos Skinas and Damianos Frantzis suddenly lose whatever reality they had in the early volume. A number of characters, either nonexistent or of minor interest in the first book, appear and are given much attention by Theotokas. It is as though, with the dramatic part of the novel successfully concluded, Theotokas wants to return to his chronicle of the younger generation's development, ignoring completely the fact that *Argo* had by this time developed its own aesthetic demands.

Alexis and his friend Manolis Skyrianos, the president of "Argo," compete for Morpho, who is frightened by the sexual attraction she feels for the young Notaras. She thinks of him as someone like Keats, and her instincts are sound: he will become a great poet and die young. When she rejects him for the safer, more manageable Skyrianos (supported in this by her parents, the well-defined Antigone and Francisco Delatolla), she does something for which she cannot forgive herself and abandons her husband shortly afterward, unable any longer to accept her retreat into what she interprets as security; she refuses to live the rest of her life with the compromise she made with her fears.

Nikiforos's affair with Olga, Pavlos Skinas's wife, is known about by everyone in Athens and, before the attempted coup, almost threatens the minister's career. The young writer, however, can no longer deceive himself that he will be a great artist; he leaves Greece, abandoning a pregnant Olga, and goes to Paris, where he lives the life of an unprincipled rake. He blames Greece for his failure.

. . . Mean, peevish, malignant; vindictive without pride; humble without beauty; sallow-faced, sullen, poisoned, with the most insane ambitions and the sensibilities of an envious servant, Greece of the small harbors and the small ships, the small houses, the small deals, the small passions, the small, petty lives, Greece the inferno of pettiness—Horrors! How could a grand talent bear to live here? (p. 377)

As background to the major action, the Notaras brothers and their stories do not harm the novel. Where *Argo* runs aground, though, is in Theotokas's decision to divest Damianos Frantzis and Pavlos Skinas of their significance. The former, aided by a finely observed Sergeant Pikios, escapes from prison and goes to

Russia, where he is alienated by the Soviet experiment. He returns to the West and is killed in Florence in an attempt to assassinate Mussolini, "a socialist school-teacher with imperial ambitions." By this time, though, Frantzis is a cardboard character, and we are shown this event through the eyes of Manolis Skyrianos, a man who never lived for the reader.

The major loss is Pavlos Skinas. With all the offices of government under his control, his dream within his grasp, he unaccountably backs down from the power that always beckoned him. It is difficult to accept such a total lack of coherence in a character, particularly after the clarity and definition Theotokas had managed to give him. The blurring and virtual elimination of Frantzis can be explained somewhat by his removal from the arena of action in his escape to Russia. But Skinas does not leave. Something else happens to him, and to the novel, that checks the momentum of the minister's drive to power and destroys the precision he had attained for us.

An historical character, plunging into the narrative, brings with him political actuality and destroys the fictional illusion Theotokas had created for his readers. The introduction of Eleftherios Venizelos in chapter 7, "The President," irretrievably dates the novel. Despite the interesting historical and political perceptions Theotokas provides, the entry of the great Cretan is an intrusion into the world created by the novel. Stendhal may have thought politics in literature was like the shot of a pistol during a concert, but that is a statement that can be interpreted in a number of ways. For some concerts, and plays, a pistol shot in the audience might be a good thing, and many novels, mediocre or otherwise, maintain their interest for us because of their political content. The problem here is this: confronted with historical facts, the reader's sense of fictional reality is distorted by the onrush of factual reality. It is impossible for Skinas to maintain his identity before such an event. He pales, as figures on a screen pale when the cinema is flooded by sunlight. Without consistency of character, he no longer determines his own destiny and becomes a plaything of a preconceived plot, his actions determined by an arbitrarily chosen structure.

Argo, thus, is a deeply flawed book. Theotokas was much too close to his material to be able to separate the political events going on around him and the rich complexity within him. He could have written a novel in the great European tradition, but his first major effort seemed to wobble out of his control. *Argo* lacks not only architecture but consistency in execution. It is as though a different man wrote about the affair between Nikiforos Notaras and Olga Skinas and the attraction between Morpho Delatolla and Alexis. The former relationship is hurried and unconvincing, whereas the latter is sensitive and true. Theotokas is particularly effective when writing about women—by no means an easy task—and his analysis of Morpho and her mother, Antigone, is impressive indeed.

Beyond all this, however, is the implicit comment he makes about Greece and the environment that he considers destructive to creativity and greatness. Though these ideas may be suspect when expressed by Nikiforos Notaras, that unwinged Stephen Daedalus, we see that something is wrong with Greece, possibly the "tragic fate of the Greek race, the weight of the great name, the idea of the insignificance of Greece in the intellectual life of the world"; possibly even the great desire on the part of the youth to do something great, to get "the Golden Fleece" or to be responsible for "creation, Renaissance, glory. . . ." Whatever the reason, something happens to Greek youth, Theotokas seems to be saying; something occurs to blight their promise or to destroy them. Nikiforos, Alexis, Linos, Damianos, Pavlos Skinas—all are harmed, even the stable Manolis Skyrianos. Only one victory, the poetry collection *Joy of Life,* brings posthumous glory to Alexis, but even that glory is disputed by critics. "Nothing good can come out of Greece, the black waves roar and echo within you, nothing good, nothing good. . . ."

III   *Duty of the Artist*

On November 1, 1935, Theotokas sent the novel to the printer, having completed it in Kifissia on August 6 and become thirty years old on August 14. "*Argo* expresses the numbers that begin with '2' and this is 'the book of my youth,' " he said. On February 7, 1936, Theotokas held the printed copy of *Argo* in his hand. He was rather satisfied with it. But political events in Greece were in their usual feverish state. Colonel Kondylis had just launched his successful coup and filled the jails and the island prisons. The author of *Argo* had been diverted from his course by Venizelos, who plunged into the novel. How could he possibly know that a General Tsaveas would leap out from between its covers and into political reality, this time without a Pavlos Skinas to stop him?

Theotokas was untouched and unintimidated, but Greek culture was beginning to show the effects of the primitive military fanaticism of the colonel. The periodicals of the time are a good gauge of the beginnings of an intellectual repression that became much more harsh as the Kondylis dictatorship returned King George to Greece and as the colonel was replaced by General Metaxas.

In an interview with Manolis Skouloudis in *Neoellinika Grammata* Theotokas was asked: "As long, naturally, as Mr. Kondylis is not listening, 'Are you a democrat?' " Theotokas replies straightforwardly:

I am against reactionary establishments and generally against fascism. I am a follower of democracy in its true meaning; in other words, of that political system that aspires and leads to the emancipation of the people. Because democracy signifies: people, the rights of people, emancipation of people. I believe in the people and am against every oligarchy or monarchy.

These are dangerous thoughts to be expressed in the second half of the thirties. Skouloudis pursues his question, asking Theotokas about the role of the intellectual. The intellectual, Theotokas continues, is obliged to take a position concerning social problems, but he must never "serve in the struggles of current political parties and be subordinate to the fanaticisms of the society."[7]

The artist, therefore, must not take refuge in the ivory tower, removed from the turmoils of everyday life, since, as a human being, he is a political animal. To do so would be to give up the arena to the forces of debasement that were dominating the Europe he had admired. The artist has a duty to express his ideas about man's aspirations and his surroundings. But he also has a duty to his art, which he must never corrupt into a partisan political instrument subservient to someone's political designs or ideological goals.

The artist is free to hold any political ideas consistent with his view of the world, but his talent is a sacred gift from which works of art should emerge unconstrained by the dogmas and tactics of political parties that would dictate temporary alliances or animosities. Far from being a compromise between the dogmatisms of the Right and the Left, the position of Theotokas was unvarying and unshakable: he expressed himself and his ideas as honestly as he could. If a particular work was unsuccessful, the failure was due to him, not to a system of thought or to the attitudes of a leader, or to the prejudices of a political group he accepted as his own.

CHAPTER 3

Greekness and the Crisis of Greek Culture

I Nea Grammata, *An Influential Periodical*

AMONG other things, *Argo* was to prove the reason for the break between Theotokas and the group of intellectuals affiliated with *Ta Nea Grammata* (a periodical he helped to form) and his closer identification with the editorial policies of *Neoellinika Grammata,* a weekly oriented more toward progressive social ideas.

In November, 1934, a group composed of "the three Georges" —Seferis, Katsimbalis and Theotokas, all more or less politically liberal, that is, Venizelists, demoticists, and "Europeans"—and of Thanos Soultanis and Dimitris Nikolarezis met at the home of Thanasis Petsalis where they founded *Nea Grammata,* whose first issue was published in January, 1935.[1] At first, Petsalis was to be the editor. After many discussions, however, it was decided that Katsimbalis would take that position, from which he later withdrew in favor of the twenty-five-year-old Andreas Karandonis, one of the best critics of poetry of his generation, whose studies of the young Seferis were to provide his credentials as a judge of poetry.[2]

It is important at this point to clarify the issues that led the editorial board to create the periodical that was to dominate the intellectual life of Greece in the late thirties. *Nea Grammata* was intended to be an impartial journal, "belonging to no school, hoping to reflect in its best expression the new and many-sided literary life that is being developed in Greece in the past few years." The board did not limit itself, however, to publishing new works but planned to give "a worthy place to the most significant and lively writers of the older generations and willingly to dedicate its pages to the study of past literary

times and generally to [Greek] intellectual and artistic history."
In doing this—following the traditions of Demoticism and supporting educational reform—they hoped to build a "bridge between the generations and to secure the continuation of the
Greek spirit. . . ."[3]

The editorial policy under Karandonis for the first three volumes was aggressive and social in orientation. Karandonis claimed
that Greek criticism did not exist and took Kostas Ouranis, writing in Nea Estia, to task for saying that it did; criticism, Karandonis said, was not a "Yes or a No, but a method, a diction."
The attack on Ouranis, one of the leading figures of that time,
continued throughout the year, but Miltiadis Malakasis and
I. M. Panayotopoulos also came in for their share of criticism.
Petros Haris, editor of Nea Estia, was attacked sharply for what
Karandonis considered a hostile attitude toward a Palamas cele-
bration that resulted in the special issue commemorating the
fifty years from the date of the publication of Palamas's first
poetry collection, and Haris's competence as a critic was thus
called into question. Finally, Nea Grammata weighed in against
the Academy, the perpetual target of talented youth and the
perpetual shield of tired, old writers, for ignoring the worthy
young writers like Stratis Myrivilis, Ilias Venezis, Kosmas Politis,
Angelos Terzakis, Thanasis Petsalis, and Theotokas, and for
awarding prizes to inferiors.[4]

Aside from its argumentative stance, which by no means makes
Nea Grammata unique in Greek intellectual life but which in
such reasoned terms is more important than either the bland
mediocrity of Nea Estia or the mindless hostility of other periodicals of the recent past, the journal published much of genuine
value: Terzakis's fiction, including Violet City; Triandafyllidis's
essays on the Greek language; Seferis's essays and his verse,
including "The Cistern," "Gymnopaedia," and "Stratis Thalas-
sinos," as well as his translation and study of Eliot's "Waste
Land"; Sikelianos's "The Sacred Road," and his "Eleusinian
Testament"; Kosmas Politis's Eroica and "Eleonora," which is
a section of Three Women; Constantine Tsatsos's essays on
Kapetanakis, Papanastasiou, and Venizelos; Timos Malamos on
Cavafy; the "Commemorative Issue" on Palamas that included
contributions by Sykoutris and Sikelianos; a chronicle of the

"Commemorative Year" by Katsimbalis; and the first poems of Odysseus Elytis, including *Orientations*.

In the first two volumes hardly an issue was published without one, and often more, contributions by Theotokas, including short stories and essays on fiction and politics. No less argumentative here than he was in either *Kyklos* or his books, Theotokas seems to be preoccupied by the same problems. But the times are more threatening. In 1935 *Nea Grammata* survived "one civil war, a number of coups, a strong political struggle, one military dictatorship, and one change of political system."[5] Censorship was imposed on it twice, once in the spring and once in the fall.

In "The Persecution of Demoticism," Theotokas mourns the new attack on the modernization of Greek education by the adherents to the *katharevousa*, supported by a reactionary government that sought to design a "New State"[6] by destroying ". . . every civilized achievement and, especially, every educational progress, submerging our people again into ignorance and corruption, into intellectual and spiritual poverty, so that it would better serve the landowners, the usurers, the demagogues, the frauds, and the princes of the House of Glücksberg."[7]

Theotokas's wrath had been aroused by the dismissal of professors like Delmouzos, Lorenzatos, Bëes, Theodoridis, and Apostolakis "like doormen" because they were identified with the demotic movement.[8] But this was not the only reason for his fury: no group of intellectuals, no newspaper, no periodical "dared protest this new attack on Demoticism and the persecution of demotic scholars" except Kostis Palamas. It must be immediately apparent that the situation was reminiscent of Greek society's behavior when Pangalos set up the gallows in Syntagma Square and threatened to hang people for crimes performed before his coup. The Students' Company, as mentioned earlier, was the only group to protest this; the rest of Greek society accepted Pangalos's barbaric law with fatalism.[9]

Theotokas must have been an awkward man for Karandonis to have around. After the establishment of the Metaxas dictatorship in August, 1936, *Nea Grammata* postponed publication until October, and Theotokas's political contributions terminated abruptly.[10] Instead, he was given a regular column in *Neoellinika Grammata*, a weekly founded by Kostas Eleftheroudakis in

April, 1935, and directed, after the withdrawal of K. Karthaios, by the brilliant Dimitris Fotiadis. In this periodical, which was an excellent mirror of progressive thought, both literary and political, Theotokas was given all the latitude he could expect under the prevailing conditions to discuss the problems that interested him. With men like Terzakis, Karagatsis, Politis, and Theotokas rallying to it, the weekly increased in scope and interest as the years of the Metaxas dictatorship wore on, while *Nea Grammata*, as a defense against the steady pressure to refrain from political commentary, withdrew from its marginal interest in social commentary and became the journal that introduced surrealism into Greek cultural life. Seferis, certainly, continued to contribute; Elytis became more active; and Engonopoulos, Embirikos, and others were introduced to the Greek reading public.

The main issue that seemed to divide the two periodicals was the definition of "Greekness," namely, how what was uniquely modern Greek could be distinguished from the cultures of Europe and the Near East. This had been a problem to the Greek even before the establishment of the modern Greek state, but generations previous to the intellectuals of the thirties did not seem to be threatened as much by questions of national identity. Perhaps it was because the Generation of the Thirties (which had not been the first to be educated in or oriented toward Europe) grew up in a postwar world that had become rapidly internationalized. Unlike their fathers and grandfathers, who left Greece for Europe, the men and women of the thirties (most of them at least bilingual) felt that they were part of an increasingly fascinating and compelling Europe. Apparently, this caused a crisis in the sense of what was Greek. Greek tradition, demotic or otherwise, seemed pale indeed after Paris and London. It would have been imprisoning—a virtual guarantee that they could never catch up to Europe—if they were forced to adhere to the rigid definitions of what their elders considered "Greek."

The *zeitgeist* seemed to demand a preoccupation with the "issue of Greekness." *Nea Grammata* approached it theoretically and apolitically,[11] while *Neoellinika Grammata* saw an exaggeration of the Greekness issue as chauvinism of a particularly threatening variety, since it aped the ideological nationalism of the other totalitarian countries of Europe.

Theotokas's belief that English literature was "the most significant in the world" must be viewed in light of this background. In his essay on Dickens, he applauds the fact that the novelist reaches the masses, and he reminds his readers that Papadiamandis, the "most Greek" of Greek writers, was influenced by Dickens and Dostoevski. It is not bad to be influenced by Europe, he claims; it all depends on which countries the influence comes from. "I believe, as a matter of fact, that the most honorable title to which a novelist can aspire is the title of European with its deeper and most noble meaning. But all this is another story."[12]

Theotokas, however, would be able to dismiss this "other story" for only so long. Three months later he returns to the discussion, maintaining that the Generation of the Thirties has been the most influenced by Europe, but particularly by the English. French influence had always been strong, while Russian, German, and Scandinavian influence began at the turn of the century. "Mistakes" will be made he continues, but "localism" and an exclusive interest in tradition are bad.

... We will emphasize, besides, that we are not about to deny our nationality or to disregard the value and significance of our Greek tradition. All of us are Greeks, bred in the most Hellenic of homes in Free or Unredeemed Greece, and our ambition is to write Greek literature. We will accept "locale" and "tradition," not like rigid or dogmatic definitions but like creative elements, which will continue to be meaningful with the understanding that they will be relevant to the aspirations of humanity and capable of reacting to, and absorbing the fruitful influences from, every direction.[13]

Civilization and culture have always developed with cross-fertilization. The ancient Greeks were sailors who knew other lands and peoples, he continues, the Renaissance began with commercial travelers, El Greco himself was not satisfied solely by Byzantine influences and needed Greece, Italy, and Spain in order to develop fully. Nations that have shut themselves off from foreign influences have withered: the only results of local and national exclusivity are "sullenness, narrow-mindedness, envy, and enervation."[14]

In October, 1937, Andreas Karandonis began to publish in *Nea Grammata* a two-part critical assessment of the work of George Theotokas that resulted in their disagreement and the novelist's complete alienation from the journal he helped to found.[15]

Karandonis's treatment of *Argo* was basically just, even though he judged the first novel by never-quite-formulated criteria that placed those spiritual opposites, Balzac and Dostoevski, on the highest footing of the genre. He commended Theotokas on his use of language. "Seferis in poetry and Theotokas in prose have clarified our demotic speech," he wrote, and compared the first novelist with "Solomos ... Makriyannis ... Psycharis, and Dragoumis" in his use of "the panhellenic demotic speech." Theotokas, he continued, was the connecting link between a triumphant Demoticism, represented by Stratis Myrivilis, and "the tradition in the process of being created now, which has as its aesthetic goal, the establishment of the novel" as a form.[16] He was critical, however, of Theotokas's use of a prologue in "A University Dynasty" and of his inability to give scenic immediacy to his writing, particularly in the Nikiforos Notaras and Olga Skinas affair.

The problem is more complex than this, however. Ignoring an occasional suspect generalization,[17] the reader still detects a point in the essay where Karandonis ceases to discuss *Argo* and touches on the personal character of the novelist, making moral judgments and indulging in psychoanalytic commentary, which may have been offensive to Theotokas.

For example, he cast doubt on Theotokas's "life force," comparing him unfavorably to Karagatsis. "Theotokas rushes toward life to conquer it," he wrote, "solely with the passion of enthusiasm, but he quickly tires, is disappointed, and, in order to save himself a possible disaster, returns quickly to reflection, to the idea of art, to his ambition to write a book."[18]

Karandonis became even more personal later. In discussing what he claimed was Theotokas's weakness in description (specifically of scenes in the Zappeion and the law school), he said:

... Theotokas lived his student's life ... not as a future novelist but as a conscientious, conservative, and *orderly* [Karandonis's italics] scholar, very regular in attendance at lectures and tutorials, yielding to the private character and the peculiar assessment of the university professors, with a developed sensitivity, with a mind open to noble dreams and with the intellectual expressions of a somewhat exceptional adolescent. ... His four or five years at the University were spent very nicely, very normally, without adventures, virtually without strong, dangerous feelings. ... [19]

Is this literary criticism? Does it have any place in a serious discussion of fiction? Later, Karandonis used the phrase "organic weakness," and the reader is not certain whether he meant it to refer to the novelist himself or to his powers of imagination, since he claimed that Theotokas was unconvincing because the events he wrote about were recent. [20]

Again, and here Karandonis was rather clear, he read into the fictional personage certain suspect conclusions about the novelist's character.

The course of life symbolized by the fascinating decline toward the pleasurable life of waste and thoughtless adventure [of Nikiforos Notaras] which the *sensual* [Karandonis's italics] Theotokas would have wanted to follow ... [is] like the statue that is erected in the National Garden, to glorify the memory of the great poet Alexis Notaras, symbolizing the wish for posthumous glory of the writer himself. [21]

Finally, with all the good will in the world, the reader must insist that Karandonis's criticism of *Argo*—which has proved to be the final word on the writer's career, even in the opinion of people who have never read Theotokas—is inadequate for yet another reason. Karandonis criticized Theotokas's work for being intellectual rather than emotional, a chronicle of disparate events rather than a fusion of myth. He was, according to the essay, a "critical" and "theoretical" novelist rather than a "creative" or "Dionysian" one, yet Karandonis nowhere proved to his reader that novels should be the latter and must never be the former. To do this, one must first define the novel, explaining what is meant by "dionysianism" in the process. Merely to

accuse Theotokas of being unimaginative is an admission that
one's critical position is no more than impressionistic.[22]

II   *The Aesthetics of Pericles Yiannopoulos*

There must have been a break between the two men by this
time because, as stated earlier, Theotokas had ceased to contribute to *Nea Grammata*. His name was never mentioned in
the pages of the journal. It remained for the publication of the
commemorative issue on Pericles Yiannopoulos, beginning with
the fourth volume, to provide the excuse for the open breach.

Pericles Yiannopoulos, that most interesting personality of the
turn of the century, had written many articles for the newspapers and periodicals of the time. Despite their hortatory and
didactic nature, these articles are almost always interesting and
frequently delightful. He struggled to inform and convince the
Greeks that their traditions were totally ignored both by foreigners, over whose achievements and values they fawned, and
worse, by themselves, and he insisted that these traditions were
important and valid and beautiful. He pleaded for a sober and
responsible criticism, which he considered a necessity for any
nation, but particularly for one as new, and as old, as Greece
about whom everyone—foreign and native—thought he knew
everything that was to be known yet knew very little.[23] This
criticism, when it comes, must, he insisted, be based on a
thorough knowledge of, and respect for, the modern Greeks. No
valid comment can be made about Greek history or Greek ideas
if it does not proceed from a deep awareness of present Greek
society; thus the interpretation of Greek civilization from Homeric
through Byzantine to modern times by European scholars is
called into question if it is not based on a wide knowledge of
modern Greece. The Greeks, in order to discover who and what
they are, must turn their backs on European speculations and
study *themselves*.[24]

Dependence—he goes so far as to call it "slavery"—on European
models and attitudes has meant that the Greeks have misinter-
preted their past and thus cannot possibly understand themselves. Greek music is misunderstood because the only living
link with the past, Byzantine ecclesiastical music, is ignored.

The Greeks, he claimed, were not even aware that there was a connection between ancient, Byzantine, and folk music. Foreign scholars, by their own specialized interests, had succeeded in convincing the Greeks that their own past was compartmentalized and airtight. Besides this, the Greek as consumer preferred the cheap imitations of European fashions in clothes—both military and civilian—and household furnishings, to the design and color usage of Greek originals, both folk and high culture. "Don't you, too," Yiannopoulos asked,

have the right to start a *mode* even in your own country, even in your own home? Why must you be *slaves*? Start from your house and throw them away one by one and replace them with Greek things, until little by little we have succeeded in throwing everything away and created, all of us, a world as beautiful as our land, our mountains, all the art work of our people, and have dressed up everything, from the cradle to the grave, with the lovely, graceful light and color and design of Greece.[25]

Yiannopoulos's major attack was reserved for the long essays on Greek art, and it was here that he made his most interesting and perceptive comments, as well as his most anti-European statements.

Greek artists, Yiannopoulos claimed, lack the originality and the courage to break away from the European masters they have studied under and imitated. They have ignored the reality that spreads out before them every day, blind to the Greek body and facial type, painting "Germanized faces on Germanized bodies." Not only is the subject matter of their Homeric, classical, Hellenistic, Byzantine and klephtic past ignored, but the very colors of the Attic landscape are unrepresented in the work of contemporary Greek artists. Yiannopoulos argued that they had actually not seen Greek color or light but had employed the same palette that they learned to use in Europe.

Europeanism, as imitation, is not progress but retrogression. Progress is the emancipation from every imitation, the freedom from every slavery, the turn toward nature. There lies truth, there life, there reality, there *creation*, there *originality*. . . . Travel the whole world, but do not become slaves. Remain free men. Don't rush to Europe looking for a *Master*.[26]

Basing himself on his ideas of ancient aesthetic theory, he rejected European art and music, particularly the German, "an expression of spiritual anxiety, illness, passion, disease, death." Greece, he insisted, is "the Orient." As his good friend Aristos Kambanis reminisces, Yiannopoulos "got the idea that it was preferable for the Greeks to accept the art techniques of the Chinese in painting rather than that of the Europeans," whose art and architecture "humiliate nature with [their] power and bulk." Ancient Greek art, on the contrary, was "like a natural blossom on a rock, in harmony with its environment as a face with its body."[27]

There can be no doubt that much of what Pericles Yianno-poulos said is of the highest value; one can readily believe that a man of such flair, originality, and self-confidence would arouse a great deal of animosity among the men he criticized. A number of reasons contributed to his highly unusual suicide in 1910 at the age of thirty-eight, but certainly his failure to imbue his countrymen with his lofty ideals or even to arouse their interest in these ideals was one of the causes.[28] The impact of his ideas was far-reaching. Ion Dragoumis in his political theories, Angelos Sikelianos in his poetic vision, and Angeliki Hadzimic-hali in her view of Greek folk handicrafts are considered to have been influenced by the aesthetic ideals of Pericles Yian-nopoulos.[29]

For his purposes, however, he had to run counter to the influence of Europe, as well as to the generations of thinkers, before and after him, who would look to Europe for guidance. The Orient would be the last place the Greeks of his time would look for cultural influence and racial identity, since the "oriental" was specifically what the Greeks were fleeing from, that upon which they blamed all of Greece's problems and her backward-ness. Yiannopoulos was bringing the latest "European" message, the greatness of Oriental ways of perception, to a land whose intellectuals had not quite digested the conflict of classicism and romanticism and were totally overwhelmed by a feeling of cultural inferiority to Europe.

The special issue of *Nea Grammata* on Pericles Yiannopoulos was published at a critical time in Greek cultural history. There was certainly nothing improper about the periodical's collecting and publishing the scattered articles Yiannopoulos had written more than thirty years before. In its first issue, as a matter of fact, *Nea Grammata* specifically stated its intention to give "a worthy place to the most significant and vivid writers of the older generation and willingly dedicate its pages to the study of past literary times and generally to our intellectual and artistic history." But the "Greekness" issue, a burning one throughout the short life span of the modern Greek state, had risen once again because of the political and intellectual climate created by the Metaxas dictatorship, whose slogan for the "Third Greek Civilization" (comparable to those of both the German and Italian varieties of totalitarianism) revealed the attempt to mold the national character along certain guidelines.

III   *Attacks Against Theotokas*

Aristos Kambanis, a man who had figured earlier in Theokas's life, became Professor of National Indoctrination under e Metaxas regime and director of the ideological organ of the ourth of August party, *To Neon Kratos*. There is no indication at all that he had any hand in the creation of interest in the life and work of Pericles Yiannopoulos, though he had been the protégé of the writer in the early years of the century, nor was there any connection between *Neon Kratos* and *Nea Grammata.*

Kambanis's periodical was less literary, more political and conomic, its articles running to theoretical studies of corpotism, Marxism, Western parliamentary decline, and friendly nalyses of Salazar, Franco, Hitler, and Mussolini. The periodil began in 1937 and grew larger and more successful as the cade neared its close (while *Nea Grammata*, incidentally, began clining), though editorially it began to show some concern out its political orientation as the war broke out and neared eece. Mussolini's invasion of Greece, of course, threatened ideological foundations and it stopped publication in Febary, 1941.

No political significance must be read in the decision of *Nea rammata* to publish the Yiannopoulos commemorative issue t the time Greece was being subjected to the edifying improvements of Greek fascism. His hostility to Europe, however, could only be viewed with concern by a man like Theotokas, who had so much spiritual and intellectual affinity with Europe. He was, like most of the Generation of the Thirties, a *European* and he found nothing wrong in taking Europeans as his "masters." In culture, he would insist, one could have a master without necessarily being a slave.

The Yiannopoulos attack on Europe, as justifiable and as healthy for Greek culture as it may have been at the turn of the century, was exhumed at the wrong time. Yiannopoulos, moreover, used unacceptable journalistic epithets about Europeans in order to make his case stronger. At any other period—say, only four years earlier—Theotokas's reaction, such as it was, would probably have been more favorable. He would certainly have caught the spirit of much of Yiannopoulos's irony and sarcasm. Yiannopoulos's insistence on the creation of a new Greek civilization, however, one that rejected centuries of European culture as "diseased" and "barbaric" and insisted on a sterile and confining nationalism, could not be viewed in 1938 as anything but the sort of jingoism that provided an aesthetic foundation for the doctrines of fascism.

Theotokas, in an article published in the competitive *Neoellinika Grammata,* was restrained in his assessment of Yiannopoulos. Objecting to his being considered a deep thinker, considering him little more than a journalist, Theotokas feared "that this glib, uninformed and irresponsible Greek-worship obscures even more our already obscure literary and artistic conscience." Yiannopoulos's preference for the newspaper *katharevousa* revealed his inability to understand Demoticism, and his choice of Gyzis, whom Theotokas considered an example of Munich academicism, as "the purest expression of Greek ideas and sentiment" compelled him to dismiss Yiannopoulos as an art critic. Yiannopoulos's rejection of Trikoupis as a statesman, his advocacy of a National Theater that would avoid all non-Greek plays, his "demagoguery" and "didacticism" led him, according to Theotokas, to the worst kind of narrow nationalism that could consider the Europeans "barbarians." This was dangerous, he concluded, because "in our days . . . [it is] an intellectual lesson for the new generation," while a century before this Dionysios Solomos had said that the Greek nation "must learn to consider *national* whatever is *true.*"[30]

Neoellinika Grammata devoted a full issue of commentary to the Pericles Yiannopoulos commemorative, and Fotiadis had asked contributions from a wide variety of intellectuals, including Karandonis. Fotiadis, in his editorial column, stated that he liked Yiannopoulos's style but found it unconvincing and hysterical, having little of the "Greek sense of measure" the ancients possessed and having more in common with the "European decadence" he so hated. It is Fotiadis and not Theotokas, as Karandonis claimed, who casts doubt on the manner of death, considering Yiannopoulos's suicide "staged." The most meaningful articles in the issue were those by Angelos Prokopiou[31] and Karandonis himself, who thought that Yiannopoulos's aesthetics "could have and should have been expressed" only in Greece. He thought that Yiannopoulos's work would have helped create a criticism based on modern Greek criteria. (Karandonis might have found this confining, since he always referred to European art as standard, as we saw particularly in his criticism of *Argo*, which he found inadequate in comparison to the works of Balzac and Doestoevski.)

If a genuine neo-Hellenic philosophy—humane and not humanlike [?] is created one day, it will show the influence of Pericles Yiannopoulos's work. Let the young, who now philosophize, read him with passion and love. The manner in which he considered and expressed the most burning problems of our race, and especially his ample Hellenism, will be valuable to them as a saving dike that will help save their souls from being drowned without hope of returning to mother earth in a vain and scholastic terminology of European university thought.[32]

It is clear that, even ignoring the elaborate, and mixed, metaphor of inundation, Theotokas and Karandonis were speaking a different language. How different can be seen in the personal attack the editor launched in the pages of *Nea Grammata* against Theotokas. In "The Collapse of an Intellectual," Karandonis selected Theotokas as the only one to speak against the Pericles Yiannopoulos commemorative issue, with an article he characterized as being an "incomprehensible, dizzy, hollow libel," one in "bad faith . . . which only his spineless friends would possibly applaud." He went on to interpret this critique as "a childish resentment against our periodical that dared publish a critical study that had reservations *about only one aspect* of his prose work." How else could this behavior be explained, he asked, than that it is a result "of a mental perversion and an intellectual slackening that recently more and more weakens the talent of Mr. Theotokas, that dilutes and causes it to fade, and that changes his well-known seriousness and the soundness of his thought to unrestrained negation?"[33]

Karandonis found this "decline" and "literary weakening" mirrored in everything Theotokas had written recently, and implied that Theotokas "abandoned" all his ideals when he discovered the "great public." *Argo* had gone into a second printing, despite Karandonis's criticism.[34]

Theotokas's only reply to this barrage was a calm letter to Fotiadis in which he reprinted a few of the comments made about him. He questioned, moreover, the good faith of anyone who would respond so forcefully and passionately to criticism and who would "systematically attack any person who refuses to become his tool and who wishes to retain his independence of judgment."[35]

If Theotokas did not defend himself, Angelos Terzakis and Dimitris Fotiadis defended him faithfully. The editor of *Neoellinika Grammata* considered himself of the "European Greek party." He was proud of the ancients, though he would never forgive them for their total lack of interest in "Greek color" and "Greek light," important issues upon which "we" the moderns are "whizzes."[36] But the ancients were universal men and not localists; when he saw, moreover, that none of the important cultures denied that a great share of their art and inspiration had come from other nations, it would be "comic for us with our still poor civilization to turn our backs on everyone and head off by ourselves toward . . . Sahara!"[37]

Terzakis was more personal, defending Theotokas's criticism of Karandonis's and Katsimbalis's attempts to present the Yiannopoulos commemorative as a symbol of "total modern Greek dogma," imposing it rather than proposing it. He voiced a criticism often made of *Nea Grammata* in the Fotiadis journal, namely that Karandonis had lost his way ideologically and aesthetically. "He began by being a great admirer of Palamas, then got involved with European surrealism, and finally became a supporter of a grim chauvinism."[38]

Karandonis defended himself by citing *Nouvelle Revue Française*'s publication of writers as diverse as Valéry, Claudel, Gide, Breton, and Eluard and accused Fotiadis of trying to capitalize on the discovery of Pericles Yiannopoulos by *Nea Grammata*. His journal presented texts, he said, while *Neoellinika Grammata* presented violent attitudes; however, this was not just, since, besides Karandonis's own study and the fine Prokopiou analysis, virtually all the articles were enthusiastic, some even hysterically so.[39] Only Fotiadas, Theotokas, and Panayiotopoulos were critical, and Theotokas was less harsh in his choice of words than Fotiadis.

The personal issues tended to obscure the deeper problems dividing the Greek intellectuals of the time. The other side of the Greekness problem was the problem of Europe, as Yiannopoulos knew, but the intellectuals of the Generation of the Thirties had another problem to face: which Europe? The Europe of the West, the parliamentary Europe that looked to the increasingly threatened Paris and London, or the Europe of the brown and black shirts? It would be wrong to say that the "European Greeks" like Terzakis, Karagatsis, Fotiadis, and Theotokas were not interested in "Greekness." A brief acquaintance with their work will show that their genius is inseparable from their sense of racial and national identity. Greekness, Theotokas insisted, was not self-adulation or local color or vague comments. "The whole issue is whether we are able to cultivate in our country a certain kind of man, whether we can develop into awareness and cultivate a certain ideal of life."[40]

Published when it was, however, the Pericles Yiannopoulos commemorative smacked of the all-too familiar chauvinism and the hostility to anything foreign that was an everyday matter in Nazi Germany and Fascist Italy. It is a pity that the rediscovery of Yiannopoulos's work and its publication in a superb issue resulted in a personal conflict that poisoned the relationship between heretofore good friends and polarized the Greek intellectual community until the eve of the Second World War.

CHAPTER 4

Shorter Fiction:
The Coming of World War II

I Euripides Pendozalis and Other Stories

THE years immediately preceding the Second World War were fruitful ones for Theotokas. After his break with *Nea Grammata*, he became a steady contributor to *Neoellinika Grammata*, producing a series of weekly articles in "Chronika," a special column that permitted him a wide range of subjects. It was during this time that Theotokas published the collection *Euripides Pendozalis and Other Stories*,[1] and two novellas, *The Daemon* and *Leonis*, the last quite possibly his best achievement in fiction. "Euripides Pendozalis," the title story of the collection, and *The Daemon*, might be considered by-products of his long preoccupation with *Argo*, but *Leonis*, a superb account of adolescence in a world of cataclysmic international events, reveals the mastery of the novella form Theotokas might have attained if he had repressed his interest in the large, orchestrated novel.

The character type of Pendozalis had always interested Theotokas, possibly because there was such a great difference between the serious, reflective novelist and the driven careerist. As is only proper, we do not meet Euripides in Greece, where his restlessness and ambition would be blurred by the native luxuriance; we meet him abroad, in the ideal laboratory conditions of Brittany, where people are sober, trusting, and phlegmatic.

The narrator and two friends, students at the Sorbonne, go to spend the summer in the north, preoccupied as much by pretty, barelegged girls in sandals as by the eternal Greek problems: the overwhelming Greek tradition and the "silence of the centuries." It is here, appropriately in St. Malo, the pirates' home, that they meet Euripides Pendozalis, a mixture of dreamer, self-proclaimed genius, and pathological liar. He claims to have done everything and been present at all the significant events of Greek and world history, and he boasts of having met Ghandi in India and George Bernard Shaw in Italy and of having psychoanalyzed Freud in Vienna. He is now betrothed to a French girl whose father he defrauds by charging everything he buys to the respectable M. Blondell's account.

That Pendozalis is a liar the three young men are well aware. He owns Mount Psiloritis in Crete and his family, claiming descent from a famous Byzantine clan, is friendly with Venizelos, who goes to the Pendozalis library to translate Thucydides. It is clear to the young men that they are dealing with an adventurer whose behavior might harm the Greek name, but they vote two to one against informing the Consulate about the danger. Besides, Euripides is not an ordinary opportunist: he is driven by the "nonexistence" of the Greek and personally tries to make up for the "silence of the centuries," traveling tirelessly in Asia and Africa, toying with the idea of going to Hollywood to become a scenario writer, and attending lectures at the Sorbonne, where he seems to have had a mystical experience while listening to Léon Brunschwicg lecture on the "rationality of algebra and the algebra of rationality."

The narrator and Pendozalis meet only briefly then separate but continue to see, or hear about, each other as they pursue their own destinies, the former a stable and sober businessman, the latter a meteor flashing across the sky. The narrator, just entering commercial life in London, receives an invitation to the Ritz for dinner from Pendozalis, whom he had last seen going off to Spain in the luxury automobile of a towering Prussian woman. Pendozalis misses Greece but is annoyed by the modesty of the Greek achievements. He wants the Greeks to do something great, something astonishing and complains that "we have wasted almost twenty centuries doing hardly anything, if you exclude that careerist El Greco, who pretended to become a Spaniard in order to catch hold. And still we're wasting time" (p. 59).

When the narrator asks him why Greece should "do something," Pendozalis answers: "To laugh. . . . It would be funny. . . . We'd laugh a lot." But since Greece did nothing, Euripides Pendozalis is next heard of from Brazil, where he creates a sensation in Rio with a series of lectures on "the eternal Greek spirit" and on Greek culture. In the lectures, he lies about the "Renaissance" Greece is experiencing, describing the various schools of philosophy and sociology that make Athens once again the beehive of intellectuality it had been.

If a different reality still reigned in Greece from that in Rio, so much the worse for us. Euripides was certainly not to blame for doing what he could for the common problem. Greece was to blame for not being able to follow him with the same spirit and imagination. (p. 56)

Pendozalis ends his life in Cephalonia, a man defeated by reality, "harmed" by France, where he was involved in *Le Comite grec,* a group of Greek gamblers who were reputed to control gambling at various French casinos. His sister is trying to find him a wife, and he is angling for a position. Euripides Pendozalis, when the narrator last sees him, is on his way to becoming a petit bourgeois.

It should be clear that Pendozalis is the spiritual brother of Nikiforos Notaras, the ambitious Greek who found Greece too small and had to go abroad to find the opportunities his restlessness demands. The theme is a major one and almost totally unexploited in Greek fiction. Theotokas attempted it a number of times, but all his other attempts can be considered relatively unsuccessful. Petros Halkias in "The Lake" and Yerasimos Ieronomatos in "Simone Was Her Name"—both stories from the collection in question—are from the same mold, ambitious men of action who ignore their rich interior world for the treadmill of history.[2] "Euripides Pendozalis" is Theotokas's only successful handling of this theme, probably because he employed a narrator who saw the events through his own perspective and provided the reader with a point of view by which to judge his major character. In other stories, we are shown the characters in all their blind actions without being filtered through a more interesting and intellectually complex mind.

It is this tension between story and character, or subject matter, and the form that Theotokas employs to contain it, that will characterize his efforts for the next few years. The tension is most noticeable in his novellas, because it is in these that the writer feels most strongly the need for a narrator with a specific point of view and a recognizable character. In his large-scale novels, *Argo* as well as the future *Invalids and Wayfarers,* the central consciousness is the omniscient narrator, delving into his characters' minds, witnessing their most secret as well as their most public acts, commenting upon their failures and triumphs. His short stories, most of which were written in this decade, are either sketches or a sequence of sketches that gain their power from sharply perceived scenes, as in "Childhood," or they are fairly externalized narratives, as "The Lake" and "Simone Was Her Name." The unique "Everything's in Order" allows him to act as the limited third person narrator who accepts the fact that the minds of certain of his characters are not available for his commentary.

In "Everything's in Order" and in a three-part narrative to be discussed later, Theotokas reveals a great sensitivity in detailing intimate and delicate matters that his political-intellectual interests almost succeeded in hiding. In *Argo* we were given indications of this in his treatment of Morpho and Antigone Delatolla, but "Everything's in Order"[3] is a brilliant execution of a theme that Theotokas totally ignored later.

This is a triangle story that pits the love of Martha Diamandopoulou for Ismene Nikodimou against the threat to this probably unhealthy relationship posed by the dull Mr. Karambatsos, an engineer with a contempt for the intellectual and artistic life. The two girls dream of going off to Paris together and of becoming involved in the cultural life of Europe. But the engineer breaks into these illusions with the force of reality. The social pressures are there, particularly for a girl like Martha whose parents have lost much of their money in a recent economic crisis. Girls of their time and place must marry, the mother of Ismene tries to convince her visitor, and "mediocre men are always handier in that dark issue called happiness. The others, the exceptional men, even if they aren't deceivers, are fantastically bothersome." Great loves are rare, she assures her, and not always pleasant. "Marriage, housekeeping, children," particularly with a man as sober and dull as Mr. Karambatsos is reputed to be, "are the only solution" (pp. 184–86). Predicting that Martha's marriage would separate them, Ismene asks her not to leave. Martha has feared the scene and has postponed her decision to Karambatsos for two months, but when she thinks of the life she would give up by fulfilling her "duties" to marry, she rebels and decides to refuse him. Martha's decision is the right one, the reader feels, while knowing that it proceeds from the wrong motive.

The fateful interview between Martha and her suitor is a splendid analysis of feminine psychology. She is prepared to refuse him until he reveals weakness and uncertainty; he does not want to make her life unhappy or hateful, he says. Does she love someone? She loves no man, Martha replies, knowing he could not possibly understand her words. In the end, Martha agrees to marry him, and Theotokas convinces us totally of the reality of her about-face; she wants to break the hold Ismene, her quiet but powerful friend, has on her. She is tired of her imprisonment; she is also desirous to know what the rest of society and "civilization" mean by love and marriage. Her decision comes from despair and from a demand for freedom of action. Her marriage to Karambatsos will be disastrous because the two have literally nothing in common and, since we know she will be unable to bear his philistine insensitivity, will fortify Martha's basic attitudes toward men. Because Ismene will remind Martha of the culture and sophistication from which she is now barred, marriage will appear to be a trap, the tax one pays for keeping a vulgar, materialistic world functioning.

"We are not happy," Mrs. Nikodimou, Ismene's mother, murmurs to herself after the girls have left her. Marriage is a trap, and love, that wild beast, lurks outside it, threatening the bourgeois structure. "Everything's in order," Theotokas concludes. "Just as long as there isn't another economic crisis soon. As far as everything else is concerned, the world is in order" (p. 208).

If Theotokas did not write another story like "Everything's in Order," his three sketches—"Therapeia" (1932), "The Gang" (1936), and "The Garden with the Cypresses" (1937)—collected under the general title "Childhood"[4] came close to it in delicacy and sensitivity. Almost a preliminary version of *Leonis* and, like it, having none of the basically sentimental perceptions of childhood as being an age of security and innocence, Theotokas's three sketches document the growth of a boy from a perplexed childhood to a troubled adolescence confronted by the mysteries of love and death. Like *Leonis*, again, a boy, the central character of childhood, sees the chaos in himself mirrored in the world outside, a world darkened by the shadow of the Great War.

II The Daemon

Coming immediately after *Euripides Pendozalis and Other Stories*, *To Daimonio* (The Daemon),[5] a novella published in 1938 and given the Academy of Athens's Prose Award in 1939, introduces the reader to the Christofis family. There are a number of excellent qualities in this novella, not the least of which is Theotokas's choice of the point of view of a narrator. As we noted in our discussion of "Euripides Pendozalis," the central narrator becomes a crucial consideration in the novellas Theotokas wrote during this decade. With *The Daemon*, Theotokas shows that his instincts are right in his selection of a central consciousness.

Pavlos Damaskinos is a sensible man, limited in the way logical men are, unable to understand extraordinary people and ideas. He is not insensitive, merely unimaginative, the ideal foil to an erratic, volatile, and confusing family of characters who are inhabited by the "daemon" of the title. His meeting with the Christofis family—in whose members a "wind of madness" and, its corollary, genius, circulate—opens him to love, to pain, and to a sense of life's mystery. Because of his encounter with them, the stable and smug Pavlos experiences a creative disorientation that enriches his life and deepens his self-awareness. The fictional Euripides Pendozalis provides the relatively characterless narrator with a sense of how men of flair respond to a dull and unchallenging reality. Pendozalis is always in focus and without him the story would be flat and pointless. We cannot dismiss Pavlos Damaskinos from *The Daemon* so easily, however, for it is through his perceptions and assessments that we respond to the Christofis family.

The mother, daughter of a great shipping clan, is a vague, withdrawn woman who wanders through her garden, glasses perched on her nose, a basket dangling from her wrist. The father, a mathematics professor at the gymnasium of the island (obviously Chios) is considered mad by his students. But Jean Martin, Pavlos's counterpart, a sober young Canadian with the British Archaeological Institute, is convinced that the professor is a genius. Pavlos, who has been in the old man's class, knows that Christofis does not teach but merely calls students to the blackboard and quizzes them indiscriminately. Or else he covers the board with cabalistic symbols that are incomprehensible to the students, forgetting often that he has a class before him, breaking the chalk, then writing again—frequently on the cornice and along the walls—until the bell rings. Does the Christofis family have "genius"? Pavlos knows better.

These are fairy tales. . . . We know each other very well on this island. There are no geniuses here. There are just a few insignificant and senseless provincials who dream of making a great name and doing startling things and, because they don't find the way of startling anyone, become neurasthenic and melancholy. This is all the mystery there is of the Christofis and other families that I know. (p. 44)

Something, perhaps the genetic combination of the two, has produced three talented but unstable children. Pavlos's friend, Romulus, has definite opinions about God, the soul's immortality, the language problem, society, love, and marriage; the only unresolved question in his mind is what he will do with his life. He wants to write poetry and to be a mathematician. Perhaps he'll write mathematics in verse? In the old days, he says, "men lived in conformity with their imaginations, while we have separated our fantasy from our lives. That's why we suffer" (p. 14).

He suffers, certainly, from a wide variety of moods, sometimes violent.

At certain times I feel that I am suddenly seized by a power higher than logic and will. And not only I but all those near me, everyone in his turn. You remember my father at school . . . in those moments the daemon took him. A daemon plays with us—how funny, really! Plays without plan, takes us, leaves us . . . enjoys itself. But nothing will come of all this, I know. We are a company of unfortunates, lost in *t*he depths of a dark province. There are moments . . . when I want to reach the limits. (p. 51)

But what the "limits" are he does not know. Pavlos, certainly, does not understand his friend, questioning Romulus's use of the phrase "dark province." Isn't he aware of their island's beauty, of the clarity and brightness of the Aegean? It is with these stereotypes that Pavlos tries to confront the questions that torture his friend. Pavlos likes poetry, too. "It seems to me the most polite amusement men have found to rest their spirits from the struggles and worries of life." Poetry, he loves particularly, "in [his] hours of relaxation." He inquires of Romulus: "What are your poetic plans?"

Pavlos Damaskinos would never have known about suffering if he had not met Romulus's younger sister, Iphigenia, a woman of passion, beauty, and talent, who intoxicates him. The first time he is alone with her, Pavlos proposes marriage. "I would very much like to . . . make you happy," he says. "The truth was," he continues, "that at that age I was unable to speak to a girl about love without mentioning marriage. It was impossible for me to think of another solution." She rebuffs him harshly. "What is it that you [people] see in me? . . . I don't want love. I don't need your hearts. . . . The world is full of beggars. . . ." And the stable Pavlos senses despair for the first time. "I sense rocks within me, everywhere, hard, sun-scorched, sharp. My life was rocks, like my island, a pile of dry rocks in the midst of the sea. I walked on rocks. I climbed over rocks, with effort, with bitterness and without hope. And I was nothing but a beggar" (p. 70).

It is Thomas, the youngest, who will realize his genius, not as a singer, the study of which art takes him to Western Europe, but as a world-famous surgeon. By that time, however, the family has ceased to be a unit. The old man, leaving a manuscript full of gibberish that seeks to explain the secret of life, asks Pavlos to burn it in the fireplace. When he dies, the islanders pay him great homage. Romulus goes to sea as a wireless operator, locks himself in the radio room, and sends an S.O.S. for no conceivable reason. The next morning, the captain sees a number of vessels bearing down on his ship, breaks into the radio shed, and finds Romulus dead of natural causes. Pavlos, after seven years in London with his family's shipping concern, sees Iphigenia acting in a French drawing room comedy in the provincial city of Volos. He goes into the seedy theater, recognizes her voice immediately, and remembers the great power of her wasted talent. "She was like a bird of the storm, tamed and trapped in a modest cage." As he watches her, he thinks: "[This is] the woman I love. It is she and cannot be another. . . ." But Iphigenia is ill and her past has caught up with her. There is such a sadness about her that Pavlos, out of love and compassion, proposes marriage again. She refuses him a second time, implying that her past is too great to be ignored. "I belong to everybody," she says (p. 118).

The Christofis family, because its outlines are not blurred by a large novel's orchestration, is much more successfully delineated than its counterpart in *Argo*, the Notaras family. The novella's form compelled Theotokas to focus only on the essentials of his narrative. In this he was aided inestimably by his choice of Pavlos Damaskinos, the sober, self-effacing man as the narrator. Certainly no genius, he had all the traits of that great mystery, the average man—capability, conventionality, health.

We must recall that Pavlos, too, has left Greece, but he could disguise his longing by calling it "business." He marries the daughter of a sea captain turned ship owner, a fellow islander, and consolidates his holdings after his father-in-law's death, developing a large shipping company. He "transferred" to Greece to give his children a good Greek education. His wife and he get along well. No passion, no romance, just a sound, solid marriage, "like our island ancestors," he says. He never speaks to his wife about Iphigenia, with whom he spent the night in Volos and never saw again. He is busy gathering books for a commendable nautical library and preparing to write a "broad study of the history of contemporary Greek merchant shipping, which is . . . the most interesting expression of the practical activity of the Greek people" (p. 121–22).

And we recall Romulus's comment about men in days of old living "in conformity with their imagination, while we have separated our fantasy from our lives. That's why we suffer." The suffering of the Christofis family was obvious. Perhaps for that reason they were considered mad; or perhaps it was because of their suffering that they were brilliant. The suffering of average and healthy men like Pavlos Damaskinos was less obvious because it was deeply buried.

It is he, ultimately, who holds the novella together, giving it weight and substance that it could not claim merely on the strength of the Christofis family. They are a covey of exotic birds, rare creatures made believable because of their proximity to Pavlos Damaskinos. Without him, *The Daemon* would not have the undercurrent of loss nor would it convey the feeling that much of life is inexpressible and unrealizable; that, in the final analysis, life is mysterious.

III   Leonis, *a Novella*

As the Second World War began to approach Greece, Theotokas found that the memories of his childhood were very much more complex and troubling than he had indicated in the three sketches mentioned earlier. First, there was the matter of the persona. In "Childhood" there was no obvious attempt to *fictionalize*, though there must have been modifications of reality, exaggerations, changes in perspective, and reinterpretations. As long as Theotokas had not settled on a character whose point of view contained his own personality, name, and history, he was inhibited from entering into the purely imaginative world. Once he chose Leonis as the main character of the novella of the same name, Theotokas was liberated from chronicling the actual, despite the resemblance in social class, interests, and personal history the author may have shared with his fictional hero. With this novella, the thirty-four-year-old Theotokas, certain of the coming of a war more terrible than the first, resurrected his youth and with it the bourgeois world of Constantinople in the decade between the beginning of World War I and the Asia Minor Disaster.

There are many anticipations of *Leonis* in the work that Theotokas published in *Neoellinika Grammata,* including a number

of complete chapters. In an interview, Theotokas seemed to
be aware that he was in a race against time. He wrote *Leonis,*
he says in a "note" to the October 26, 1940, issue of *Neoellinika
Grammata* because he "heard the war approaching." The book
had just been printed and was about to be released. Two days
later, of course, the Greco-Italian War began, and *Leonis,*
though "published" in 1940, bears a 1946 copyright date.[6]

In many respects, *Leonis*—Theotokas's best work—reminds one
of Joyce's *Portrait of the Artist as a Young Man;* both novels
chronicle the development from childhood to early manhood of
boys who are consciously representative of their nations. But
Constantinople in the first two decades of the twentieth century
is a much more chaotic and complex city than Dublin, and the
immediate fate of the Greek people was to be considerably more
brutal than that of the Irish after their "Troubles." First of all,
Constantinople was the Imperial City, the enticing Queen after
which scores of conquerors had aspired and many had seized
and enjoyed. Then again, it was a cosmopolitan city, full of
various nationalities and religions, as well as extreme differences
between social classes. Though the Greek community dominated
the commercial and cultural life, it nevertheless shared the
Turkish-controlled city with the various other communities, being
perhaps much more restrained, for historical reasons, by the
Ottoman authorities. Their national consciousness, because it
was more of a threat, was repressed by the Turks, and Leonis's
grandfather created a flurry among his daughters and the house-
maids by singing the war chant "Black is the Night on the
Mountains" and speaking about politics a little louder than
was wise. They were Greeks, everyone knew that, and Constantinople, despite the fact that the Turks had controlled it
for 450 years, had never ceased to be a Greek city. Only by
formality was it non-Greek. But, according to the saying, "Again
with years and times it will be ours." And the time seemed ripe.

The Great Idea was about to become a reality, the Greeks
were certain; the awakening was at hand. With the Great War
that theatened as soon as Leonis was ready for school, the
centuries-long dream would certainly be fulfilled. Leonis and
his young friends played games in Taxim Park, and, on the day
after the guns of August sounded the beginning of the world

war that all reasonable people thought would be the last, they played at war.

However, since they are filtered through the consciousness of Leonis, the sounds of war come to the reader only as a distant rumble. It is his perceptions that chronicle it for us: the German, Austrian, and Turkish armies, bayonets glistening, march through Constantinople; schools are taken over as barracks; the art school, directly behind his grandfather's house, becomes a garrison, and Leonis, when he goes to water his grandmother's flowers, sees the Germans with shaved heads, walking around in their pajamas; the Kaiser comes to inspect the Turkish and German armies in the city that had seen Basil the Bulgar-Slayer, Nikiforos Phocas, John Tsimiskis, Manuel Comnenos, and the unfortunate Constantine Paleologus. Perhaps for this reason Leonis is not particularly impressed by the Kaiser. Only tangentially do we learn the frightful cost of the war: the German soldiers Leonis sees in the streets are younger now, almost of school age. One generation has been virtually destroyed, but Leonis fails to consider this. He is awakening to that other force in life, his own sexuality.

Once he sees two women fighting in a path at the park and asks a friend what caused this dispute. The answer was *corte*, "love." Another time he and Dimos, a schoolmate, go off to the "forest" of Taxim Park and see Pavlos Proios and a pretty girl staring at each other, silently. Pavlos "was serious, he read much and was respected by everyone. He often walked by himself or went with students older than himself and discussed the ancient Greeks or the Byzantine Emperors. Leonis loved him but was shy and had never spoken to him" (pp. 25–26).

The question in Leonis's mind that he does not quite ask is: what could a serious person like Pavlos Proios, who reads much and is respected by everyone, see in a pretty girl to stare silently at her for so long? What is this *corte* that everyone knows about and of which only he seems to be ignorant? One day, Paris, another friend, brings his sister Nitsa along and the three go off to spend Sunday in the park. They stroll and talk and listen to music. After this experience, Leonis loses interest in playing in the park. He, too, goes off on long walks by himself.

Helene Phocas is his great love, but she is the ideal of every boy in the Twelfth Scout Troop, from Pavlos Proios down to the youngest, the absurdly named Mentor, who confesses his love to Leonis. "That's enough," Leonis says, infuriated. "You're still reading Xenophon's *Anabasis!*" "Am I," the child asks, "the only one who has no right to love her?" In fact, the unofficial title of the Twelfth Troop is the "Helene Phocas Troop," but she toys with them all, deigning to talk or be kissed by the younger boys only if there is no one better around. One day Leonis sees Pavlos and Helene in the park kissing passionately, and this leads to a fist fight between him and his erstwhile hero, who at first refuses to fight because he is three years older than Leonis. "You're crazy," Pavlos says and Leonis cannot disagree, for he "did not know at all why he did what he did; he did not understand himself." After that incident, he does not greet Helene when he sees her on the street.

It is with Julia Asimaki that Leonis has his first erotic experience. They take art lessons from a Professor Gaetano Montefredini, whom Leonis hates because he does not allow him to paint from nature but compels him to do still lifes with fruit or copy plaster casts of Apollo Belvedere and the Venus de Milo. Montefredini, a well-observed minor character, has a habit of ranting in front of his class about amateurs who are taking over the art world, but Leonis has a difficult time attending to his own work let alone listening to his professor. Julia Asimaki exposes her calves to Leonis, making it impossible for him to draw a straight line. She introduces Leonis to the mysteries of love before being shipped off to Egypt by her brothers and married to an Alexandrian.

The war ends one silent day. When Leonis, by now a young man, completes the gymnasium, he will go to Athens and Paris. The affairs of the world seem to be getting settled at last and reasonable men of good will can again begin making plans. Wilson, Lloyd George, and Clemenceau are in Paris at that very moment establishing the League of Nations. The past, with all its problems of war and injustice will be forgotten; the future, full of freedom and comforts, beckons.

Every nation will look to its pleasure, will enjoy its life without restraints, will walk without obstacles on the road to progress. The

Greek nation had to make one small effort still, to give one small push to settle once and for all the open business it still had pending in Asia Minor. Afterward, no other problem will arise to disturb the good life and the games of the children of Odysseus: "You are happy," the older people said, "because your life is beginning now. Fortunate generation!" (p. 76)

After the defeat of the Central Powers, the Greeks of Constantinople have more freedom. On Greek Red Cross Day a fair is held in Taxim Park with music provided by a Greek naval band and a visiting American jazz band that causes a sensation. Leonis is wearing a Greek uniform, inconceivable in the old days, and believes that "the new generation [will lead] the way ... toward a new and better world, a world of freedom and joy" (p. 95).

Leonis discusses literature with his professor, a Frenchman who tries to convince the young man to forsake Greek and write in the language already perfected as an instrument by Chateaubriand, Ronsard, Balzac, and Stendhal. But Leonis must forge the conscience of his own race in the smithy of his soul, and the hammer he must use is the still developing demotic Greek. To use another language, Leonis believes, is to deny one's own country, but the professor insists that Leonis can retain his Greekness, the quality of his nation's genius, and still use another tongue. The ancient world, he is told, used Greek; the medieval, Latin; the modern, French. Writers of all ages who had rejected their own languages did so because they viewed writing as a way of communicating with other men and preferred to use major, international languages that were already molded and formed by great intellectual traditions. Leonis considers himself a cosmopolitan, but his language unites him tightly with his nation.

You have no idea how great my joy is when I want to write a couple of lines and sense that I am handling a fresh, new, unformed language, that I can mold it as I want, that I am taking part in a very great event, a labor destined to live for centuries, even millenia, the development of a new language—and that this new language is as Greek as was the language of Homer! (p. 157)

But the "little matter" still unresolved of the Great Idea and the unredeemed Greek lands looms over the horizon. Leonis, unlike Stephen Daedalus, cannot develop in his own way. He is a child of his century. Before going off to Smyrna, Pavlos Proios tells him: "The only thing that truly counts [about understanding a century like theirs] is to enter into it, to take part in it with whatever forces one has. To involve oneself with the century, that is the issue. . . ." (p. 131).

But Pavlos is killed; Helene Phocas marries a much older man; Asia Minor is lost in the flames of Smyrna; and Leonis and his family leave the Imperial City for Athens, whose whiteness defeats the artist in him. Having given up painting, he wanders aimlessly, not knowing what to do with himself, uprooted from his past until he discovers another past and finds his place in it. He hikes in the mountains of Attica, considering his fate.

> Before, I was happy. . . . Before, I had forgotten everything, now I remember everything. Before I was young and strong; now my youth is being lost. I am double, I am two selves and don't know which of the two is more real. I am a yes and a no. . . . Something that dies and that tries to be reborn. . . . I am marked by all the contradictions of my century. I am a child of my century, a seed of history (p. 177).

Athens is the new Greek destiny. Younger and more provincial than Smyrna, Alexandria, Thessaloniki, and Constantinople, Athens is all that Hellenism has left that is exclusively Greek. It is the reality, however, that Leonis and his generation need to confront. At the novella's end, turning back from the hike in the mountains, Leonis returns "to the city where a new life awaited him," no longer a specific and very real young man, but the Greek struggling to find his way in the role that fate after the 1922 Disaster had thrust upon him.

Leonis is the final and definitive statement that Theotokas was to make about the emotional impact on him of the loss of his homeland. Other writers of the Anatolian littoral—notably Ilias Venezis, Stratis Myrivilis, Tatiana Stavrou, Pavlos Floros, Fotis Kontoglou, and Thrasos Kastanakis—were also contributing at about this time to the Asia Minor theme with works that attempted to recapture the quality of a life forever gone. Like many of the writers of his generation, Theotokas was responding to a profound need to make his peace with the theme of the loss of homeland before the arrival of the war he knew was soon to engulf Greece. *Leonis* is the tangible proof of his liberation from the "sorrows of *Romiosyne*" ["Greekness"]. With this novella, he purged from his subconscious the vestiges of his grievance with history, exposed them in the sunlight of the conscious, and freed himself for other interests.

It is no mistake that Leonis understands at the end of his hike through the mountains of Attica that he has a double self, one composed of "a yes and a no," a self "that dies and tries to be reborn." Theotokas sensed that with the coming of the Second World War, he would be further bound to Greece and further removed from Constantinople. Leonis, in turning toward Athens, "the city where a new life awaited him," was doing what Theotokas himself had done, accepting the decisions of history at his most profound and unreachable subconscious levels.

Having accepted his inability to return "home" to Constantinople, he must also come to terms with the irrevocable loss of "the City" as a spiritual home for Hellenism. During the Axis Occupation that was only months away, and at first through another genre, drama, Theotokas would attempt to recreate the lost religious center in his life. *Leonis* is the final, and melancholy, farewell to the splendid and holy city of Byzantium and the firm acceptance of a new life for himself and his nation, a life of subdued ambitions bereft of "great ideas."

CHAPTER 5

The Man of the Theater

FOR the Greek writer, the four-year Occupation was, in retrospect, a time of gestation. The post-Disaster era had forced the Greek artists out of their provincialism and compelled them to confront a Europe vibrant with experimentation. The Generation of the Thirties and even older writers like Nikos Kazantzakis and Kostas Varnalis, found themselves less interested in the native traditions and more apt to find their inspiration in foreign (i.e., European) sources. This continued throughout the decade of the 1930s, despite the worsening political climate that might have tended to alienate the Greek intellectual from a Europe slowly drifting toward totalitarianism and war. With the Metaxas dictatorship, the Greek writer found himself firmly under a totalitarian regime, and, with the Italian invasion in 1940, he was irrevocably in a state of conflict that was to last virtually a decade.

It was during the Occupation that most Greek writers seemed to withdraw inwardly, not only into themselves, but into their national traditions as well, finding sources for their inspiration in the collective past of the modern Greeks. Men like Theotokas and Seferis, who objected vehemently to what they considered limitations of a national "canon," began in this era the serious and fruitful job of creating a canon of their own. Seferis, in his fine essays reevaluated Theofilos, Makriyannis, and *Erotokritos*, while Theotokas, though interested in the same issues, devoted more and more of his attention to the theater.

Few Greek writers were as aware of the social importance of literature as George Theotokas, and it is clear that his lifelong interest in the society of modern Greece was eventually to mature into a powerful and cultivated preoccupation with the theater as an institution profoundly rooted in its culture.

86

If the novel is a social document privately apprehended, the play is a social document publicly witnessed. It requires the efforts of a large number of dedicated people, a text capable of more than private interest, and an audience not too far behind the taste of the producing company. Theater nurtures and trains an audience to appreciate and, eventually, to support by its frequent attendance, a series of performances that become a tradition. It is from this common background that a regional or national theatrical tradition is developed.

In order that the audience identify with, and want to support, its theater, it must feel that the works produced, aside from being pleasurable, are relevant to its needs and valid according to the reality by which it feels surrounded. More than most art forms, therefore, theater is an institution whose impact is measurable daily, or nightly, and which is directly dependent upon community support. The responses it demands of the audience are social and are expressed publicly. As a result, it must never be too far in advance of its public. Its values are thus more a gauge of the social mores of its audience than are those of the more private arts.

In an institutional sense, however, the only tradition (a word used with caution, since its validity is questionable) modern Greek theater can be said to have is classical drama. But ancient drama and its conventions have been a constant source of trouble for the modern Greek dramatist. Instead of being an enriching supplement to a nation's dramatic fare—as occurs in most countries—classical theater, for obvious reasons, has been one of the major obstacles to the emergence of contemporary drama in Greece. There have been dramatists, certainly, aware of contemporary trends in Europe and willing to risk experimentation, but for a number of reasons the theatrical audience in Greece has—at least until the Second World War—been characterized more by a reverence for a splendid past isolated from their own experiences and mores, than an interest in a present that speaks to them with all the confusions, weaknesses, and tensions of modern frailty. Because the Greek theatergoing public gets its sense of the lofty from the ancient tragedies it attends in great numbers, its entertainment from the review or boulevard farce, and its sense of current problems from the European and American plays that are produced by the score during the winter, modern Greek drama encounters more than ordinary difficulty in making itself relevant and important.[1]

In searching for a workable modern Greek theatrical style, Theotokas allowed himself the intellectual freedom to investigate every possible manifestation of the culture. In common with his friend George Seferis, Theotokas had a fondness and respect for the folk and native traditions; unlike him, however, he experimented in his own works with genres of the popular culture. This he began to do during the Occupation, after the ideological dialogues on Greekness that occurred in the middle to late 1930s, and he worked his way toward an attempt to use the forms of the *karagiozi* shadow-puppet plays and the humble comic-idyll, which was influenced by French vaudeville.

There must be a reason why a romantic drama such as *Morpho* has retained its great popularity despite the contempt of the intellectuals, Theotokas states. Perhaps it is because the public sees in this play a reflection of its own values. This was not an unexpected aesthetic position for men of the Generation of the Thirties, who insisted on the validity and beauty of *Erotokritos,* that other popular and much criticized work. Besides the romantic epic, which Korais dismissed by characterizing it as "suitable for servant girls," there was the "folk genius" of men like Makriyannis and Theofilos. Theotokas's theater would tend toward this.

I *Historical Plays:* Night Falls, Revolt at Anapli, Byzantine Night

The first play that Theotokas attempted, though not a product of his interest in the folk tradition, involved a theme that later emerged as a significant one in his work. Except for the rather negative references to religion in *Argo,* the attraction for the nonrational is never present in his earlier works. With *Night Falls* (1941),[2] however, Theotokas documents a new awareness of a mystery that is not explainable in ordinary terms.

The scene is the Praetorium of Pilate on the Sunday after the Crucifixion of Jesus. Pilate has tried to save Jesus, knowing that Procla, his wife, is attracted to the Rabbi's teachings, but the High Priests insist and Pilate, like a good administrator, considers it wiser to sacrifice the blood of one man than to risk civil disturbances. His secretary, a Greek-educated intellectual, is certain that there is no religious revival in Judea, because he has seen no manifestation of metaphysical interest. The earthquakes during the last forty-eight hours, however, make everyone uneasy. Besides, the marital tension between Procla and Pilate is intense, for she has fallen under the spell of the mystic East. Pilate can escape into his work, but Procla, lacking his comforting preoccupations, must confront the magnitude of her incompleteness. "Help me to forget," she tells him. "Give me your disbelief." But he cannot, and she is left much more attuned to life's terror and mystery than he. Both feel their age and the chill of evening descending upon them, but Pilate forgets this in his plan to build a network of roads for Judaea. He fails to understand her when she says that a "new kind of music" has been "born in the world." At the end of the one-act play, when she admits that she would like to die, he is too busy to notice.

If this first effort revealed an unexpected undercurrent in Theotokas's thought, the subsequent plays show him struggling to create a form that would enable him to deal with the themes presented to him by his interest in theater. He used the form of classical tragedy on occasion, he used the historical pageant, he used the comic-idyll, and finally, he used certain aspects of the folk theater which Fotos Politis had been promoting in the 1920s and 1930s, and for which he had been criticized by a younger Theotokas.

The first result of this was *Revolt at Anapli*,[3] a drama written on the model of ancient tragedy, dedicated to Angelos Sikelianos, and read to him at his home during the early and most distressing stages of the Occupation.

Although performed only once, this work, set in Nauplion in 1831 and involving the assassination of Capodistrias by the two Mavromichalis brothers, is full of compelling action, important ideas, complex characters, interesting dialogue, and a chorus that, despite its stiffness as a device, is used well.

Kostandis and Giorgis, the two Mavromichalis brothers, discuss their plan for killing Capodistrias outside the church of

Saint Spyridon, the locus of all the dramatic action. Konstandis, the plotter and leader, seems to be having second thoughts. He now views Capodistrias as essentially a good man, of international stature, who can speak to the rulers of Europe in their own language and assure them of the order and stability of the new Greek State.

But it was precisely because of the order and stability of the Ottoman Empire and of the desires of the European powers for an end to turmoil that the Mavromichalis brothers, and the Greeks in general, had revolted in the first place. By opposing Capodistrias, Konstandis and Giorgis stand for a continual, perpetual revolution whose goals seem to be the ultimate freedom of man from all bonds. Capodistrias, on the other hand, stands for a completed revolution and an orderly state, with all the restraints and safeguards this entails. To succeed in his structuring, Theotokas must characterize the brothers not as primitive clansmen with limited ideas of freedom, which they undoubtedly were, but as ideological desperadoes who are prepared to ignore the welfare and power of their clan for the freedom and dignity of all men.

Though in abstracting and generalizing, Theotokas may falsify history somewhat, the major issues in the play are significant and interesting in their own right. Capodistrias advocates the centralizing and unifying force whose ultimate goal is the education and modernization of Greece; his enemies, now that the Turk has had to give up one small portion of his still-great empire, are the local and separatist interests whose loyalties—to both clan and commerce—appear to supercede the ideals of national unity. The chorus calls on President Capodistrias to tame the wild separatism of the clans and of the fleet of Hydra; in order to do so, however, he must impose taxes on their shipping and restrictions on their privileges. His enemies insist that he has taken away their personal liberty, the freedoms of the press and of elections, while the President claims that they do not know that a state entails some limitation on total freedom.

To impose order on the recalcitrant Hydriot fleet, Capodistrias is compelled to ask for help from his allies—Russia, France and England—whose ships are still in Greek waters. The threat of Greek defeat by the superior fleets leads the admiral to destroy his ships, an act he defends by claiming that he has merely performed his duty. Having defeated Turks and Arabs on the seas, he does not see why he should allow other foreigners, now that Greece is free, to defeat him and sully the national honor. Both men are right, according to their own understanding. Capodistrias uses the foreign fleets as his instruments, as the fleet of the "Greek state," while the Hydriot admiral still holds to his beliefs in a local, "clan" law.

Those listening to the debate of the two great men reveal that they are incapable of understanding what divides them. They are perplexed by the complexity of the issues and are swayed by the most recent speaker. What is clear is that the conflict between national and regional systems, both using the concept of freedom as their slogans, cannot be resolved by the characters in the drama. The Mavromichalis brothers can no longer postpone their decision to kill the president, and Capodistrias dies, a tragic hero who has tried to lead his people to accept a value system for which they were still uneducated.

Obviously, a drama written in 1942 with this particular subject matter must be viewed in the larger political perspective of its time. Theotokas himself claimed that he sensed the beginning of civil war during the early part of the German Occupation. In conflict with the narrowly local interests was the demand that the Greek State, with the goal of modernization, democracy, and justice, be firmly affiliated with the democratic nations in their war against the Axis powers. Realism demanded alliance and, Theotokas seems to imply, even intervention for the establishment of order within Greece.

But reality is more complicated than these constructs, for the Mavromichalis brothers were champions of intensely local patriotism, the Hydriot seamen of nascent finance capitalism, while the civil war that was brewing was to be seen later by the Greeks as a conflict between erstwhile allies who intervened in the affairs of Greece.

Byzantine Night[4] marks the second attempt by Theotokas to use the form of ancient tragedy as a vessel for his thoughts on statecraft. As in *Alcibiades,* completed twelve years later, the ready-made vehicle, instead of liberating him to say things unique to his subject matter, dictated the meanings he was to distill from his work. *Byzantine Night,* as a result, though set in the court of Theophano, is strongly reminiscent of Aeschylus's *Oresteia* (with a few dashes of *Macbeth* and *Hamlet* where appropriate) and is an historical "problem" play whose questions are, by and large, posed in terms of its Byzantine context.

Romanos, Theophano's first husband, was killed, at her behest, by Nikiforos Phocas, the present emperor, who, according to a messenger, has just crushed the Arab forces at Antioch. Tired of Phocas, Theophano compels her young lover, Tsimiskis, to kill the returning king and become emperor of a Byzantium that stretches from the Balkans to the Nile and Mesopotamia. Phocas, wearing the "red shoes" that remind one of the carpet that Clytemnestra (the other "Lakaina" of tragedy) spread before Agamemnon, returns to Constantinople, unhappy that he has not liberated Jerusalem and attempting to justify to himself the regicide of Romanos by claiming that the previous emperor was weak and incapable of ensuring the security and stability of Byzantium. Theophano pacifies him before he is murdered by Tsimiskis and four assassins.

The populace is furious, restrained only by the news that Svyatoslav is proceeding toward Constantinople with a vast host. Tsimiskis is called upon to save the city, but Patriarch Polyevklitos appears and imposes the church's conditions on the new emperor's elevation to the throne. He must cleanse himself of the guilt of regicide, formally accuse Theophano of leading him to the crime, and force her into a nunnery. The dilemma of Tsimiskis is that he must either reject Theophano or abandon his vision of himself as savior of the empire.

Theophano, however, has no dilemma. Her fate is decided by Tsimiskis's decision, and her central role in the play is thus called into question. She takes her own life, and Tsimiskis goes off with his armies to battle the invader, leaving the monk and the Patriarch behind to clarify and express the real issues of the play. As representatives of two differing religious attitudes, their conflict sums up the play's moral questions: the monastic order avoids compromise by evading certain issues, while the secular order, led by the Patriarch, must involve itself in, and compromise with, a morally suspect world.

These are issues, certainly, that are present regardless of time and place. The righteous doctrinaire can always fault the man whose involvement with the day-to-day world of political reality has led him to contradictions between his ideals and his practice. As the observer, Theotokas concludes the action without taking sides, but he shows how history, like a great wind, sweeps aside all the blood, the passion, the wars, and the crimes. Are all historical events ultimately meaningless? The reader is not certain what Theotokas believes; he is told, however, that Basil II will eventually appear to save the city and provide it with "the greatest moment of the Byzantine Empire."

> Because from the dung of their crimes
> flowers the blossom of a new life,
> and youth returns to do its deeds,
> youth of beautiful illusions,
> fresh and radiant,
> with its great promises
> and its artless hopes.
>
> (p. 221)

Ultimately, it is not the derivative nature of *Byzantine Night* that harms the play. Its flaw is that Theophano, who is essentially the leading figure of the drama, takes up relatively little of the play's dramatic time and, at the conclusion, is shunted aside with little resistance from her. She is overwhelmed by men who take over what is essentially her drama. The issues that motivate her seem to be vague and unspecified. Is it her passion for Tsimiskis, the younger man, whom she possesses already? Does she have a vision of the Empire the others do not have? We know very few of her ideas. The real conflict in the drama seems to be between two visions of the world: the secular one, hinted at by Theophano and other characters in the play, and the religious one, expressed by the monk from Mount Athos. Yet Theotokas does not bring these two contrasting moralities into fruitful opposition.

II *Folk Drama*

The historical plays demanded of Theotokas a great awareness of the dramatic past and the ability to mold his characters and their problems into a traditional form. The factual material dealt with, however, demanded a sophistication that folk drama could never possess. With the exception of *The Game of Folly vs. Virtue*, the folk plays come from either demotic song or from the folk tradition, and are no less prescribed, as far as their form is concerned, than the historical dramas: the characterizations, the situation, and the plot provide the playwright with the clear outlines of his task. Unavoidably, the plays themselves depend heavily on their sources.

As *Revolt at Anapli* influenced Kazantzakis in the writing of *Capodistrias,* so Theotokas in *The Bridge of Arta* (1942) was influenced by Kazantzakis's *The Master Mason.* Just as Theotokas had employed the tradition of ancient drama in *Revolt at Anapli,* in *The Bridge of Arta,* skillfully embellishing on the folk song of the same name, he worked consciously in demotic drama, a "dramatic legend in five scenes," which he dedicated to Nikos Kazantzakis.

The master mason, the protagonist of *The Bridge of Arta,* because of a series of misfortunes, is unable to complete his bridge and succumbs to the tradition that claims that the burial of a human being in the foundations of the structure will guarantee its stability. In the case of the master mason, this is proof that he is willing to sacrifice his wife and happiness for the achievement of his ambition. There is a touch of the Faustian theme here, certainly, as well as the ancient theme of hubris, a great pride that will lead him to personal disaster. But the master mason is free, despite the fact that he is confronted directly by a representative of the daemonic forces, a Shade, who demands the builder's young wife as the sacrificial victim. When he makes the decision to trick his wife into retrieving his betrothal ring from the foundation, the master mason is fully conscious of the implications of his act.

Using the folk material he had encountered in Nikolaos Politis and others about the *kallikanzaroi,* the evil and destructive spirits who roam through the Greek world during the twelve days between Christmas Day and Epiphany, in *The Dream of the Twelfth Night* (1943) Theotokas constructs a folk comedy whose charm is not quite sustained to the end, but which nevertheless retains its interest for the audience.

Kyra Kali, twice-widowed mother of Malamo and Ploumbo, agrees with a peddlar—who she does not know is Mandrakoukos, leader of the *kallikanzaroi*—that Ploumbo, the beauty who threatens to take all of Malamo's suitors from her, is to spend the night at the mill. This, she is convinced, will be a good way to rid herself of Ploumbo and help her favorite daughter to find a good match. But the clever Ploumbo outsmarts the *pagana* (the devilish spirits of ancient Greece who plague the Greeks for abandoning the religion of their ancestors for Christianity) and returns home with the substantial dowry that she has tricked the *kallikanzaroi* into getting for her. Malamo should do likewise, the mother thinks, but her favorite is not as clever. She calls on the Archangel Michael, the scourge of the devils, who saves her and reconciles mother and daughters.

The Castle of the Beauty (1944) is another folk comedy based on a demotic song. This one-act play deliberately employs, according to Theotokas's instructions, the motivations and characterization of the *karagiozi*. Set in Anatolia in a legendary time and place, sometime during the decline of Byzantium but before the final Moslem triumph, this is a shadow-puppet play with the actions and motivations of this form of theater.

The beautiful Kyra Manou is the daughter of the Duke, who has gone off to fight the heretics in Babylon and locked her in a tower under the protection of the nurse. A clever Chiot, the nurse stands between Kyra Manou and Abdousalam, the handsome Arab prince who desires her, and Tsaousis, his diabolically clever Moslem sidekick, who will be decapitated unless he can devise a ruse to capture Kyra Manou for his master. With their first disguise, as a gypsy and his bear, and their second one, as Christian monks going to Jerusalem, they almost succeed in entering the tower, but Tsaousis betrays himself each time. The third attempt proves successful.

Manou knows that according to tradition she must leap over the wall to her death, and Abdousalam offers to jump with her, but the nurse recognizes a jewel he wears about his neck: the Arab is really a Greek prince, son of the King of Trebizond, whose nurse she had been, and Tsaousis is her very own son. Both boys had been sold to the Caliph of Baghdad. Without great soul-searching Abdousalam and Tsaousis transform themselves into loyal Byzantine knights and ride off on white horses to seek out the old King of Trebizond.

Written in what Theotokas called "a fugitive mood" from the turmoils of the late Occupation, *The Game of Folly vs. Virtue* (1944) uses, in very simplistic terms, two aspects of man's personality, polarized as Virtue, or what might be called the superego, and Folly, the libido. Under the reign of the "party of Folly," the womanizing Emperor Andronikos and his advisor, Doukas, the legendary Byzantium, which is apparently not threatened by enemies outside, is confronted by an internal threat. The "Party of Virtue," led by Mavrianos, believes that the good times must stop, and that their leaders "must take a position concerning the great problems," a stance that demands "a world theory." At a banquet, the two opposing sides meet and Andronikos's sexual prowess is lauded. There is one woman in the Empire whom Andronikos cannot seduce, he is told, and that is Arete, Mavrianos's virtuous sister, who lives a retired life with only her books and old teachers as company. A wager is made (if Andronikos fails, he loses his crown; if he succeeds, Mavrianos is decapitated) and Andronikos leaves for his prey, who, warned by the legendary "Bird of Song," tricks him by changing places with her servant.

The Party of Virtue triumphs and Andronikos is put in chains, from which Arete herself rescues him. Why, she does not know, except that though she may demand wisdom and virtue and proper behavior, she cannot live in a world that has totally imprisoned or done away with Folly.

III *Theotokas As Administrator*

The Occupation and its vicissitudes had left the National Theater in a critical condition. The star, Eleni Papadaki, had been executed by the EAM-ELAS for collaborating with the Nazis (a theme that was to occupy Theotokas in *Invalids and Wayfarers*), the actors and actresses were either too young or too old, and the building itself had been seriously damaged by the fighting during the street battles of the December revolt. This was the situation when George Theotokas was appointed general director for two years with an executive committee composed of new men like Kanarakis-Roufos, Panayotis Kanellopoulos, K. Karthaios, Theodores Synadinos, George Seferis,

George Katsimbalis, and Nikos Hadzikyriakos-Gyka. Angelos Terzakis was director of dramatology and Pelos Katselas and Socrates Karandinos were directors of performances.

This new group took over its duties on February 16, 1945, and planned to begin performances in the summer or autumn. P. Exarchakos, general director of the Government Accounting Office, however, with a bureaucrat's zeal, demanded that the theater function at once rather than place him in the awkward position of paying "employees for doing nothing." To appease him, the theater quickly whipped up performances of Oscar Wilde, Molière, and two Greek plays, Terzakis's *The Great Game* and D. Bogris's *The Betrothal*.

The men and women of the theater were, like the rest of their countrymen, divided politically, and Theotokas was compelled to invest a major effort at smoothing over the explosive mood. Though he tried to run the theater democratically, a few older actors who were not given leading roles felt discriminated against because of their royalist backgrounds and complained to various governmental offices.

All in all, ten works were scheduled during Theotokas's tenure, including Shakespeare's *Merchant of Venice*, Gogol's *The Inspector-General*, Ibsen's *The Pretenders*, Maxwell Anderson's *Winterset*, and Armond Salacrou's *La terre est ronde*. But these plays, by their very nature as foreign works, did not contribute to the controversy that later characterized the first postwar years of the National Theater.

Ilias Venezis's *Block C* and Manolis Skouloudis's adaptation of Dostoevski's *The Idiot* were hailed as great successes, whereas Thanos Kostopoulos's *Salvation* had a more negative reception. It was to be the selection of *Capodistrias* by Nikos Kazantzakis, a writer Theotokas always admired, that was to provide his tenure as general director with the controversy that led to his release after the formation of a new government.

Kazantzakis's *Capodistrias*, performed on March 25, and Sikelianos's *Sybil*, projected for the future, were attacked by the newspaper *Estia* in its usual personal and unrestrainted style. Both writers were deplored as "Eamo-Communists" and "sickening"; Kazantzakis was considered even more "sickening than his *Capodistrias*."

At first, the newspaper *Kathimerini*, owned by George Vlachos, an old-time supporter of Kazantzakis, did not participate in this campaign, but this prestigious conservative paper later took a stand against what it called "this dynamite for the national foundations," which is what the plays of Kazantzakis and Sikelianos were considered by Aimilios Hourmouzios, under whose by-line the article appeared. As a matter of fact, *Sybil* was never performed because Theotokas was unable to find the funds to support it until the British government paid up the twenty-one million drachmas back rent for a theater in Thessaloniki that the ENSA (Entertainments National Service Association) had used. This occurred, however, on the very day Theotokas learned that the new government had released him from his position at the National Theater.[5]

Much of the difficulty surrounding Theotokas's first tenure as director of the National Theater stems as much from an ideological disagreement over the function of a national theater as from the political climate in which he fulfilled his duties. This is illustrated clearly by Alkis Thrylos (pseudonym of Helen Ouranis) in her general assessment of Theotokas's literary work. She praises his "almost" lifelong stand for intellectual freedom, qualifying her statement because she claims that "at a very critical time for the spirit, he stretched out his hand, or at least a few fingers of the hand, to those who planned to imprison [the spirit] and gag it."[6] Unfortunately, this is not clarified, and one can only assume that she means Theotokas's scheduling of Kazantzakis's *Capidistrias* immediately after the December battles. But she also disagrees with Theotokas regarding the role of a national theater, claiming that his insistence on experimental plays was incompatible with the function of the institution, which is to act exclusively as a "museum" of traditional drama.

The vision Theotokas had for theater in Greece was a grand but eminently logical one. If the National Theater in the capital city was to act as guardian of foreign and ancient dramatic traditions, another force, "the Experimental Stage," should be founded to provide a place for works whose value has not been established by time and whose technique might be less orthodox or merely less familiar to the audience. This more intimate experimental stage could well provide the ideal forum for drama by young Greek playwrights, as well as their foreign contemporaries, so that the National Theater could be assured of having a stake in the future.

A national theater and an experimental stage, however, would provide only for Athens. What of the encouragement of drama in the provincial cities and in Thessaloniki, the capital of northern Greece and the nation's second city? For Thessaloniki he had another solution, one that would need to wait until 1960, eight years after the end of his second tenure as general director of the National Theater. Since he believed that the provincial theaters should be run on local rather than national funds, he suggested that Athenian theater groups (whom he urged to use smaller stages, possibly at the ground levels of the new apartment houses that had begun to change Athens's urban features after the war) be given a tax break if they agreed to the stipulation to establish themselves for not less than a year in a provincial city.[7]

Theotokas would have the opportunity he always wanted to enrich the theatrical life of Greece when he was no longer in an official administrative capacity. It was in the latter part of November, 1960, at the home of Constantine Tsatsos, then minister to the president of the government and later president of the Academy of Athens, that Constantine Karamanlis asked Theotokas what the government could do to promote the intellectual and artistic life of the nation.

Theotokas had no need to ponder his reply. "Create a [National] Theater in Thessaloniki." In a convincing manner he discussed the probable cost of a venture of this magnitude and mentioned the names of two or three men of the theater who could undertake such an effort. An old and trusted friend of Theotokas, Socrates Karandinos, at that time director and producer with the drama school of the National Theater, was asked by Karamanlis to draw up an organizational plan and budget as quickly as possible. Within ten days, on January 13, 1961, a month and a half after the meeting at which Theotokas first proposed it, the National Theater of Northern Greece was legally established. Theotokas himself was requested to act as president of the committee for the organization of this National Theater.

In the summer of 1961, Socrates Karandinos staged Sophocles's *Oedipus Rex* in a modern translation by Fotos Politis in the ancient theaters of Phillipi and of the island of Thasos, thus establishing a summer theatrical tradition that was to begin in northern Greece on the final weekend of July and last until August 15.

Theotokas, writing in the newspaper *Vima*, tells of the astonishing success of the performances. "The people of Macedonia and Thrace . . . spontaneously, with no other exhortation but a simple advertisement" of the existence of the theater, set out in such great masses from Florina, and even from Alexandroupolis, that the organizers began to fear that the number of people would surpass the acceptable limits. "But how could anyone deny entrance to people who arrived at the theater from so far away, having taken such pains?" Once again, the patriot in Theotokas marvelled: "We saw . . . how much the Greek people thirst for real culture and high art, how ready they are to embrace and love every manifestation of high culture that is offered."

The establishment of the theater of northern Greece was the fulfillment of part of his vision for drama. Theotokas saw in the Karandinos version of *Oedipus Rex* the beginning of a northern Greek tradition of performance, one that complemented the "introverted nature and stylistic and ethical austerity that characterize[d] the people of the northern provinces." This "cofunctioning," this "identification of the characteristics of theater and populace" may create, he opined, in future audiences an understanding that the dramatic message is not something foreign to them but "an expression of their own personalities." Furthermore, the function of the northern theater was to develop and promote its own artists, who would eventually help to create a unique northern style, one that would complement and compete with that of Athens.

It is this creative competition that Theotokas mentioned in his Inaugural Address at the National Theater in Thessaloniki on June 3, 1961. Though not necessarily referring to the National Theater of Athens, he envisioned the existence of a state theater in the capital of northern Greece as a creative factor, initiating new levels of the populace into the dramatic experience and introducing them to the habit of play-going, which would help support private theaters by creating an educated, alert, and interested audience.[8]

IV *Shadow Puppetry or Comic Idyll*

The problem of theater, the crisis that it was undergoing, was due, Theotokas believed, to a number of causes. Film was frequently mentioned as a great competitor of the theater, but the Greek cinema in Theotokas's opinion, had never achieved "the power and value" it could have secured for itself because of the omnipresence of foreign films. The Greek industry was under-capitalized and primitive, he believed, and needed the cooperation of American or European management to provide it with sources of investment capital and a market for the distribution of its products.

As it stood, therefore, film was not the cause of the Greek theater's crisis. Uncertainty as to the role of state support was a more valid reason, but the most compelling one was the lack of a meaningful dramatic tradition, an issue that was related basically to the question of the definition of modern Greek culture.

There was no "modern Greek style" in theater, except for the popular entertainment as it had been "naturalized" and "Hellenized" by the people, whether rural or urban, in the form of the shadow puppetry of the *karagiozi* or the comic idyll. These native works seem to have had little or no difficulty in relating meaningfully to the public at large. The important challenge, therefore, was to attract the larger audiences that had lost the habit of theatergoing when drama had withdrawn from the concerns of the greater public and addressed the few. In giving up its ambitions, or pretensions, to universality, theater had lost confidence in its ability to relate meaningfully to the public at large. It was precisely this meaningful relationship with the mass audience that Theotokas tried to establish in his work in the theater.

In essence, the preoccupation of Theotokas, as it expressed itself in actual theatrical work in the decade of the 1940s, was an outgrowth of the search begun much earlier for what was authentically *Greek*. Current political realities in 1938 compelled him to take a critical stance against the more blatant aspects of "Helleno-latry" in the commemorative issue devoted to Pericles Yiannopoulos of *Nea Grammata*, but the Occupation and the defeat of fascism had purged any residue of chauvinism that the Greekness issue might have contained.

After his firsthand experiences as director of the National Theater, Theotokas was ready to devote himself once more to the writing of works that would permit him to test his own dramatic theories in practice as well as to address himself to the lack he felt in the theatrical tradition of modern Greece.

A comic idyll, *Encounter on Pendeli* (1947), neatly fulfilled Theotokas's desire to write intellectual comedy while using a traditional style. Working in the modern historical past, *Encounter on Pendeli* deals in a farcical manner with the era of banditry that existed in Greece in the second half of the nineteenth century. Bandits like Chryssoleondas, though the authorities in Athens may offer a bounty for them, lead a life attractive to Yvonne, a French woman very reminiscent of certain Shavian heroines. She meets the bandits and the slapstick gendarmerie who pursue them on Mount Pendeli and agrees to help Chryssoleondas capture Lord Lily, who has been pestering her to marry him, by enticing him up to the peak of Pendeli. The bandit wants amnesty so that he can become respectable and enter the social and political life of Athens before all the good jobs are taken by the young. With Lord Lily as hostage, Chryssoleondas feels that he will be able to force the Greek government, which always fears the intervention of the British fleet, to grant him the amnesty he so desires. Bristling because of the British ultimatum, the Greek leadership decides to behead Lord Lily to show its independence, but changes its plans abruptly when it is learned that Lily has asked Astero, the amazonian niece of Chryssoleondas, to marry him: it is never wise to reject important contracts with the British nobility.

The conflict here, of course, is similar to that in *Revolt at Anapli*, where the two forces in conflict are those of the state and of the local or clan group. Treated, however, in a farcical way, with generous use of costume, sprightly dialogue, and song, *Encounter on Pendeli* is a fresh and delightful look at Greek history.

More realistic than the previous "folk" dramas, *The Price of Freedom* (1948) tells the story of Katsandonis, the prerevolutionary hero who, under the sway of Ali Pasha, went to a martyr's death. This play, performed to many unfavorable reviews, employs characters who have become national celebrities and are thus seen through the perspective of a man whose ideas are not conventionally patriotic. Theotokas was bound to disturb some viewers with his interpretation of motive and actions. Furthermore, his refusal to follow the trend of the European theater and his use of the traditions of Greek puppetry were certain to arouse misunderstanding and even hostility.

Katsandonis and Veli Ghekas are opponents who subscribe, as decent men and honorable warriors, to the same code of conduct; both are destroyed by Ali Pasha, who demands that the Albanians use unacceptable means to capture the Greek klepht (guerilla) hero. Surrounded by clever and resourceful advisors and his attractive Greek consort, Vasiliki, Ali Pasha is the ideal successful tyrant, for his concern is for the efficiency of his regime, the physical well-being of his subjects, and the orderliness of daily life. In modern terms, he views the achievement of an expanding gross national product as being intrinsically more important than the liberty he knows the Greeks feel they should have.

Katsandonis stands for the "foolish" demand for national independence, while other Greeks, in or out of court, are much readier to yield to the tyrant's will. Despite the fact that the Greeks are allowed schools, monasteries, and churches, they are vaguely restive under Ali. Katsandonis's presence is therefore aggravating to timid men like the grammarian Oikonomou, who does not want to get involved with rebellion, and to the cunning Thanasis Vayias, who after years of repression is afraid of heroics like those of the klephts and instead serves Ali Pasha, using his considerable ingenuity in tracking down Katsandonis.

The final interview in prison between the cynical Ali and the idealist Katsandonis is reminiscent of Shaw or Anouilh, for the issues transcend the men as surely as *The Price of Freedom* transcends folk drama. The Greeks are bent on rebelling against an economically progressive state and an enlightened despot, whose good intentions are not promises but facts. Katsandonis insists, however, that freedom and a new, a *national*, way of life is more important than economic progress. Seeing Katsandonis go to his death as a hero of legend, Manolis Oikonomou, the timid grammarian, is swept up in a patriotic fervor, while Vayias remains unconvinced: the only way the Greeks will gain their freedom, he is certain, is by their cunning, not their courage.

V *Realistic Drama*

The only theatrical work that Theotokas set in a contemporaneous society, *Hard Roots* (1956), was inspired by his jury duty at the Criminal Court of Athens during a murder trial involving clan conflict in Crete. Here again, as seen through a number of plays, Theotokas is concerned with the conflict between a more primitive code of behavior and the law of the state. With tensions that have become familiar to us, particularly as they are illustrated in fiction, drama, or cinema dealing with other Mediterranean societies, like the Sicilian and the Corsican, *Hard Roots* confronts an outsider, Eleni Apostolou, a young Macedonian schoolmistress, with the Cretan variety of *omerta*, the appalling silence and feigned indifference of a society as it witnesses the blood vengeance of one clan against another—the Farmakis clan against the Dikaioi—in an attempt to even a score whose only outcome would appear to be the death of all the male members of both families.

The vendetta is an old one which had been revived during the Occupation, when the clans supported different guerrilla bands. The names, of course, have a political significance for Theotokas, but the drama's important conflict is between the law of the state, viewed as in most literary works as the superior and more enlightened, and the law of the clan, which is characterized as no better than primitive retaliation.

It is the silence that allows social evil to fester, and it is the police, all outsiders, and—according to the play's tensions—representatives of an enlightened state, who are compelled to struggle against recalcitrant people to see that justice is done. Eleni Apostolou should be their natural ally, for, as the schoolmistress in the community, it is her job to teach the children "to become better than their elders." The widow Kyra Pagona, who explains clan justice to the young woman, makes it clear that the villagers recognize the inability of their society to surmount its weaknesses. It is fear, however, that keeps all decent villagers silent and acquiescent.

Because of her attraction to Manolis Farmakis, Eleni Apostolou's motives become mixed and the drama loses the clarity of its tension. When Manolis hides in her bedroom, she does not turn him in; when Pagona has qualms about perjuring herself, the schoolmistress comforts her by saying that "God will understand. . . . Mistakes are human." She even justifies her own silence to the police by claiming that her value as an educator in the community—which demands trust on the part of the villagers—supercedes her testimony in a murder trial.

Her abandonment of the values she represents and which she was supposed to inculcate in her pupils is even more total as the play reaches its conclusion. She agrees to go to Africa with Manolis, who has rejected a compromise with the police director that would have allowed him a lighter sentence, and is ready to begin a new life away from the demands of a just state. Manolis, however, dies in a blaze of fire from the rifles of the Dikaioi, who shoot him down just as the couple is running across the beach to board the waiting ship.

"For us the rifles and the blood," Eleni Apostolou says, having totally accepted the Cretan value system, "the hard rocks that never let us escape, and the honor that kills." But her acceptance of these values seems to occur without a struggle, and ultimately the play fails because her character is not convincing enough to withstand the author's manipulation for his own purposes.

Since *Alcibiades* (1957) exists in an English translation (as does *Folly vs. Virtue*), it may represent the hope Theotokas nurtured that eventually he would be known as a dramatist as well as a novelist. This was not to be because of several factors: the rise of the theater of the absurd and the consequent difficulty of historical theater; the lack of interest in theater about ancient Greece; certain intrinsic weaknesses in the work itself, which is heavy with long patches of conversation, much of it intellectualized and clearly meant to provide historical background; and, finally, because of the character of Alcibiades himself.

The problem with the great Athenian is that we know so

much about him. As a man, Alcibiades seems to have gone to extraordinary lengths to define himself and his goals and has managed—through the reports we have of him from Thucydides and Plutarch—to satisfy our literary interest in him. He completes himself and needs a dramatist who is little more than biographer. For a playwright, the only solution to this problem is to concentrate on some incident in the life of Alcibiades. To make a pageant of it, as Theotokas has done, is merely to inform the reader (or viewer) about this intriguing man and to interpret him in modern historical terms.

Certainly, Theotokas had indicated that the problem of Alcibiades was never really explained convincingly by the ancients. His character, his "complex," as Theotokas refers to it, does not seem to perplex modern audiences. Theotokas, who was constantly preoccupied by politics, however, saw Alcibiades as a man driven by patriotism and ambition to the point where he identified himself with his nation. He sacrificed himself for the glory and honor of his country, but only if it accepted his leadership. If his country rejected him, he felt that it rejected itself and must suffer for its mistakes. A man who lives with this "fixed idea," his own "personal Great Idea," to employ Theotokas's phrase, is driven to realize it despite the wishes of the countrymen for whom he gives his all, and he is checked by no tradition or ideology. Alcibiades's tragedy, as Theotokas stated, was "that his vision was born too soon." Time was his enemy and his looming failure drove him to a madness that was clearly delineated on stage.

The End of the Road (1960) is set in 1905 during the Macedonian Struggle and, like most of Theotokas's serious drama, involves the conflict between two types of justice: in this case the conflict is between the secular and religious types. In the context of this three-act play, the irredentist struggle between the Greeks and the Bulgars for the rich province from which the Ottoman Empire must soon retreat overwhelms the Christian ideal of attaining union with the divine by ignoring the world of politics and leaving it to the passing Caesars, whoever they may be. The phrase, "the end of the road," here assumes a double meaning, for in the terms of Louriotis, the school director who is secretly a Greek army officer, it signifies the achievement of Macedonian union with Greece, while for the metropolitan Simeon, it signifies the attainment of the vision of "uncreated light," when one's whole being is permeated by a view of God.

Theotokas here reiterated a point he had made all his life: for the Greek, religion and nationality are fused: Orthodoxy and Hellenism are confounded in such a way that the former is subordinated to the interests of the latter. Houssein Pasha, the governor of the province, is like Ali Pasha in *The Price of Freedom,* genuinely perplexed by what he considers the Macedonian Greeks' thwarting of their own interests by opposing the Turkish rule: "You have," he says, "your patriarchates, your communities, your schools; you have all the means and all the opportunities to advance from the Adriatic Sea to the Persian Gulf. What more do you want?"

In truth, what would they have if they united Macedonia with Greece? A larger Greece, certainly, but also the gradual and unavoidable retraction of Hellenism from the Near and Middle East. A large empire had enabled the Greeks to prosper and progress far beyond the stage that a relatively poor nation could duplicate. Moreover, by retaining secular power, the Turks took upon themselves the political compromises, the tyrannies and the oppression that are the unavoidable concomitants of politics—the matters of Caesar—sparing the Greeks, who were thus enabled, theoretically, to attend to the matters of God. Houssein Pasha's defense of empire would have been a necessary intellectual effort for Theotokas at the time of *The End of the Road,* since this was the era of the Cypriot struggle for union with Greece and the case for the other side had to be given.

The plan of Louriotis, whose secret betrothal to the schoolmistress, Katerina Doukas, provides the play's love interest, is to set ablaze the half-Greek, half-Bulgar village, kill off the guerilla band of Tsakalaroff, and take away their cache of weapons before the arrival of the Turkish forces. Bombs and incendiary devices are placed throughout the village, whose residents may all conceivably be sacrificed for the patriotic struggle. By destroying the Bulgar partisan group and saving the weapons, the balance of power in Macedonia would necessarily shift to the Greeks, though at the expense of hundreds of innocent Greek, and Bulgarian, lives. If the town is not burned, however, the Bulgarians would offer battle in the open, the outcome would be uncertain, and, in any case, would take too long, which would permit the Turks to arrive in time.

As far as Louriotis is concerned, there is no moral conflict. The issue is joined, however, when he compels the metropolitan, the highest official in Greek Macedonia, to approve the order by countersigning it. Though Simeon objects, he signs the command finally, denying his Christianity and capitulating to his Hellenism. All the Greek characters in *The End of the Road* clearly choose the nation over Christ, and Simeon, who as an Athonite monk had been exposed to the teaching of the Hesychasts, goes into a trance during prayer, sees the "uncreated light," and becomes blind. Louriotis is caught by the Turks after his tactic proves successful and is sentenced to be hanged, though Houssein Pasha allows him to marry Katerina before his execution.

Influenced, as Theotokas stated, by *The Trojan Women* of Euripides, *The Final War* (1964) is an unsparing view of the suffering of the defeated and the smug certitude of the victors who believe that the war recently concluded will be the final one in history, after which man will devote his full attention to peaceful pursuits. War has accomplished nothing positive, this short play says, except perhaps to provide subject matter for epic poetry, and the suffering it has caused and is still to cause is unassessable. One by one, Hecuba, Polyxene, Andromache, and Cassandra learn of their brutal destiny, while Helen, the cause of a great civilization's destruction, will return to Sparta with her husband as though nothing has occurred. "We know today what your duty was," Hecuba tells her: Helen was to act as agent in the destruction of Troy. She is "mud," the body, evil unfleshed *because* it is enfleshed.

Before going off and leaving her alone, the Achaean officer is not distressed. "That's war," he says. "Luckily we know that this war . . . will be the last. Those who live after us will live happy days."

For Theotokas, as for most Greek writers, the interest in drama could never be the rich and fulfilling concern it should have been because of the realities of theater: production costs and uncertain audience support. The valuable experimentation he brought to bear on the form, the quality of his insights and preoccupations, and the concern for the practical problems faced by the Greek dramatists were lost because of the daily realities of stage production in Greece. There are very few writers who, like Kazantzakis, could claim to be interested in drama that is meant primarily to be read. Most authors want their work to be performed; they want an audience to confront the ideas embedded in action and dialogue. This is, after all, the meaning of communication in art. The experience of Theotokas in the theater is typical of too many Greek writers who have felt that they were working in a vacuum, unable—despite their patience, cultivation, and constancy—to break through to the national audience they felt they wanted to reach.

CHAPTER 6

The Political Animal

I *Promise of a New World Unfulfilled*

WITH *On the Threshold of a New Era,* written in January, 1944, almost a year before the liberation and the December battles, Theotokas expressed the doubts and thoughts that had preoccupied him during the long occupation. As with *Forward to the Social Problem,* written in 1932, he revealed himself to be less a Greek than a European thinker, since the issues that directly concerned him in this pamphlet were international rather than specifically Greek. Because of Greece's geographical position, however, conflicts that seemed not to be Greek initially became so with distressing rapidity.

The major preoccupation of Theotokas in this essay was the character of the new world promised, or threatened, by the now-certain defeat of the enemy, who, at the time of writing, was still occupying Athens. He recapitulated economic and technological history in his effort to place the reader "within the storm" of actuality and concluded that the current world situation was the product of capitalism and the Industrial Revolution, both of which stressed the necessity for individual initiative uninhibited by the interference of centralized power. The result, the creation of a "cyclopean technological civilization [with]... vast concentrations of wealth" had also forced "millions under an economic tyranny as merciless as the political and social despotisms the world had known in the past and [created] about themselves misery, instability, confusion, war."[1]

When socialist thought appeared "on the proscenium of history," therefore, it brought a message "full of plain and unshakable certitudes" to a bleak and despairing world. Believing in the future, full of confidence in "Man, Science, Progress, [and]

Justice," envisioning a world without war or poverty, a serene
and orderly civilization unlike the nightmares of domestic
oppression and imperialism created by finance capitalism, socialist thinkers seemed confident that their many solutions would
eventually be accepted because of their validity. The problem
with many socialist theoreticians, however, was that they did
not concern themselves with questions of a "spiritual or ethical
nature," viewing these issues as unimportant and preoccupation
with them as unproductive. But as a social democrat, as someone
always suspicious of dogmatic pronouncements, and as a man
more and more conscious of the limitations of reason, Theotokas
must caution in *On the Threshold of a New Era* that

... the desire for individual freedom is not an outmoded bourgeois
demand, a legalist superstition of the relaxed middle class. . . . Be
careful! [The desire for freedom] is deep, alive . . . burning, dangerous, beyond theories and ideologies: it is a profound instinct. . . .
[It is] the spontaneous desire of every human being for the completion of his uniqueness under the sun, for the uninhibited flowering
of his individuality within the reality of flesh and spirit. . . . The excessive repression of an instinct can result in nothing good. If it is not
effected with prudence and understanding of human nature, there
will be an awful price to pay tomorrow. . . . Be careful. The human
spirit is infinitely deep. It hides unquenchable desires and an ability
for renewal and contradictions that common sense cannot apprehend.
Do not make the mistake of enclosing it within hard rationalistic
formulas that life will upset tomorrow. Leave [some] doors open. . . .
(pp. 13–16)

In the West, technology and capital had collaborated to develop an exploitative tyranny which, despite parliamentary systems that left doors open for human freedom, had produced the
upheavals of the two World Wars and the economic depression
that the forty-year-old Theotokas had lived through. In the camp
that claimed to be socialist, on the other hand, technology and
state capitalism were creating a structure very much like that
of the West, while at the same time closing the doors the parliamentary system had left open.

Theotokas confronted the future from the threshold of a
new age and found it bleak, viewing a world he had already

seen in many of the "large industrial cities of the West" and had considered "despairing." Socialism claimed to be able to make this industrial world more just, orderly, and more beautiful, but there does not seem to have been in the new world of Soviet Russia, at least, too great a concern for the things Theotokas demanded: freedom to do what his nature demanded, and a sense, which man lost with the coming of the machine, of belonging to the universe. He agreed with D. H. Lawrence that industrialism had shattered a harmony once manifest between nature and the church.

But men and women, hesitating on the threshold of the new age, could no longer choose between industrialization and the old world, which was rooted in, and subordinate to, nature. The choice had already been made. Postwar man, bereft of the life experience of the church and unable to return to an idyllic past, was doomed to an industrialization that promised to solve the chronic economic crises that had disjointed the old world and led irrevocably to a conflict of economic classes.

The choice, therefore, was not between industrialization and the natural world of old values. Nor was it solely between the two types of industrialization—that of the West and that of the Soviet Union—although it was in this guise that the coming conflicts would appear. The choice ultimately was between two views of man: the one which conceived of him as an appendage of the machine and the other which viewed him as the bearer of the great legacy of the past, a spiritual being with concerns that transcended those of efficiency and productivity. Contemporary man required a new religious attitude that would enable him to "tame and humanize the bloated and diseased body of our society" and to find a way of embracing "Tradition and Revolution, Necessity and Freedom, the Mass and Individualism, [and] Science, and Poetry" (p. 28). In thinking about the conflicts the new era promised, watching the two ignorant armies prepare themselves for battle, a man like Theotokas could only stand on the sidelines and shout "Be careful of this" and "Be careful of that."

And, in truth, there was much of which a prudent man like Theotokas had to be careful, particularly when the future was to begin within the calendar year. Though he could foresee that a major conflict loomed over the Greek horizon as the new world emerged out of the rubble of war, he still seemed optimistic as the time arrived for the Nazi occupiers to leave Athens in November. "In the Sun of Freedom," a short statement written especially for an issue of *Nea Estia* devoted to the soon-to-come Greek liberation, Theotokas revealed his pride at the behavior of the Greeks during the Occupation and his confidence that Greek youth, combative and proud, would forge a new destiny for Greece.[2]

II *The Civil War and its Aftermath*

A great deal has been written about the Greek civil war, much of it contradictory, impassioned, and interested. The same struggle Theotokas had written about in *On the Threshold* and made to appear a solely European concern, broke out in the streets of Athens during the first week of December and pitted Greek guerilla units against British troops that were brought in especially to suppress them.

The issue was a complex one, particularly for a man like Theotokas, who had always considered himself a demoticist, a socialist, an antimonarchist, and an internationalist. The December battles and subsequent events complicated the position of Theotokas because they tended to confirm his ideological opponents on the Right about the correctness of their opinion, not, however, because his own position was proved to be vulnerable. Monarchy, the extreme Right—which had collaborated with the Nazi occupation—the financial oligarchy, and the intellectual and linguistic reactionaries were suddenly placed by the events of December, 1944, in the position of having all their predictions of a Bolshevik bloodbath confirmed.

It is this line of reasoning that Theotokas had to confront, and he did so in a brilliant argumentative essay entitled "On the Subject of Communism," published during the height of the civil war in 1948.[3] The middle class, he claimed, had always been the dominant factor in Greece, and from the Revolution of Goudi in 1909 to the December battles in 1944 had always been uncompromisingly progressive and representative of Greek society as a whole. Greece had never had a powerful capitalist class (this, of course, had been one of the ironic thrusts in the

analysis of Pavlos Skinas's career in *Argo*) and, in the nineteenth century, had quickly absorbed the Phanariot and Hep-
tanesean aristocracies.

The major factor in modern Greek society, therefore, had been
the bourgeoisie, which was a dynamic, egalitarian, and progressive force. The *Philiki Etairia*, the demotic movement, and the
Revolution of Goudi were expressions of the aspirations of the
middle class of Greece, and men as varied as Korais, Trikoupis,
Psycharis, Palamas, and Venizelos were unmistakable products
of that class. The bourgeoisie retained their ties to the village,
remembered and revered their origins, and—his most telling
point—agreed without bloodshed on the necessary redistribution
of land, a decision that had much to do with forcing Spain into
a civil war that lasted for four brutal years.

Thus, under the leadership of the middle class, Greece, according to Theotokas, was an increasingly progressive and humani-
tarian state. The December revolt, because it was a *class* struggle that threatened the consensus of Greek society and pitted
proletarians against the bourgeoisie, succeeded in shocking the
latter, separating them from their characteristic progressive
tendencies, and, as a by-product, allowing the fascist Right
to appear prescient in its excessive fear of progress. The December revolt was a proletarian revolt, in the view of Theotokas, and the civil war, which Markos Vafiadis said was being
fought for "democratic freedoms," succeeded only in giving
power to the extreme right that, as a matter of course, began
immediately to limit civil liberties.

Theotokas exhorted the middle class once again to become
contemporary, radical, and creative and asked that the state
become liberal in civil rights so that those who followed the
Communists out of various generous motives could once again
be absorbed into the mainstream of Greek life.

"On the Subject of Communism" is clearly an *apologia* for the
position of the Center as it found itself forced increasingly to
play a role in the postwar political world and to declare itself
with one side or the other. As far as the soon-to-be triumphant
Right and the obviously retreating Left were concerned, moderation was a luxury the Greek could not afford. He had to
choose between one extreme or the other.

Theotokas was having none of this, however, for he would never be prepared to take a position that violated his sense of decorum. Silence would be preferable. He spoke out, though, when he felt that the class to which he owed allegiance as a thinker and citizen was being accused of class-wide corruption and was being declared, according to Marxist ideological doctrine, potentially extinct.

The argument in "On the Subject of Communism" shows Theotokas making the most of his always interesting ability to generalize, a talent he uses here in a partisan way. Perhaps for this reason he did not include the essay in his *Intellectual Journey* (1961), a collection to be discussed in chapter 8.

Theotokas was a firm demoticist, a lifelong social democrat, an outspoken antimonarchist, and a committed internationalist, but he was also a loyal and enlightened bourgeois: he could not tolerate the fashionable romanticization of the proletarian and the dogmatically negative attitude toward the bourgeoisie that was shown traditionally by the Communist theoreticians, virtually all of whom belonged to the middle class.

The worst that can be said of Theotokas in this essay is that he chose to deal with only those facts and persons that supported his generalizations, leaving out those that might have tended to confuse or undermine the points he was trying to make. He was not, in other words, trying to arrive at an incontrovertible truth; he was trying to win an argument, to rescue from disapprobation a creative and, he felt, generally liberal and progressive social class, and to convince it to be, once again, the generous and dynamic leader of the Greek nation. If, for example, Korais, Trikoupis, Psycharis, Palamas, and Venizelos were products of the Greek bourgeoisie, so, presumably, were Kodrikas, Deliyiannis, Kondos, Cavafy, and Gounaris. To pursue this point, the same parliament (1911) that promulgated a constitutional amendment authorizing land reform, that is, the expropriation with compensation of large estates from landowners, also added Article 107 to the Constitution, which formalized *katharevousa* as the language of the Greek state. The present writer does not mean to belabor this point, and certainly he feels extremely uncomfortable placing Cavafy in the above grouping, if only to act as a contrast to the clearly demotic

Palamas. Suffice it to say that, in this essay, Theotokas went to the defense of the bourgeoisie but did not spare, at a time when it was rather awkward to do so, the extreme Right wing that tended not to concern itself overmuch with the respect for civil liberties.

The position Theotokas found himself in must be considered unenviable; yet it was a usual one for him: an antimonarchical social democrat in a country where the extremes were the Bolshevik totalitarianism he had always feared pitted against a monarchy that had eased the way for, and supported, the Metaxas fascism he had so despised in the past. These two extremes were supported by foreign powers, erstwhile allies whose expressed ideals were principles to which few reasonable men could take exception, though in practice the demands of what they viewed as their national interests forced them to play roles that were not always so laudatory. With the electoral defeat of Churchill, Great Britain withdrew support from the Greek government, and the United States, with the Truman Doctrine of 1947, became the dominant power in the Mediterranean, replacing the British who had controlled Greek destiny since the days of the Revolution. Greece, as a result, was firmly locked into a struggle between two nations, two nation-blocs, and two ideologies. It would be at least a decade before enough of his countrymen would share Theotokas's coolness of intellect to make dialogue possible.

Greece was in the middle again, or rather on the periphery of both extremes, on the border of the two power blocs, one to the north and the other—an exhausted and divided Europe (and an overconfident America)—to the West. Given the intellectual climate of the time, it is not difficult to determine where Theotokas's loyalties would lie in such a conflict, for he had been alert to the Communist threat two decades earlier and is on record for his stand. Besides this, he was culturally more attuned to the West and politically much more enamored of the transatlantic democracy than any form of government he had seen in Europe, except that of the Swiss, perhaps, who as a people did not interest him. With the tireless interest of the erudite European, Theotokas had followed the New Deal years in the United States, and as a democratic socialist had approved most of Roosevelt's policies.

Though the United States of Europe he had envisioned in the early 1930s did not seem to be a very real possibility as yet, Theotokas still considered the role of the nation-state as essentially a limited, if not a negative, one. As a Greek, the concepts of language, culture, and a common historical tradition would always be creative and fruitful ones for Theotokas, but the arbitrary boundaries, the difficulties imposed on travel and commerce, and the narrowly viewed concepts of national sovereignty were insurmountable obstacles to the development of an active and vital Europe. Since the nation-state had so obviously failed, perhaps the "continent-state" of the United States of America could offer him some insight into the European predicament?

III *Visits to the United States and the Soviet Union*

It was in the early 1950s that Theotokas traveled to the United States to write *Essay on America* (1954), one of the more perceptive and clear-eyed books on the subject.[4] His views were clarified by two factors he kept perpetually in mind: the first was the Europeans who had preceded him and whom, because of their objectivity, he used as intellectual guides, while the second were critics of America, also Europeans, whose hostility could place them politically within the camps of either the extreme Right or the extreme Left. Theotokas viewed both political extremes as antidemocratic and envious of the average American, the Right because the society of the United States appeared classless and thus without a recognizable hierarchy, the Left because the American workers seemed to have lost their class solidarity and had been totally absorbed into the general ethic. This "classlessness" was annoying to the critic of America because, according to the Right, it allowed the rapid change that undermined a traditional society, while according to the Left, it militated against a definitive change by revolutionary means.

But why should a person allow himself to give up the "profound instinct" that Theotokas had identified as "the spontaneous desire of every human being for the completion of his uniqueness under the sun," or to subordinate "the uninhibited flowering of his individuality within the reality of flesh and spirit" to the demands of a social hierarchy to which a man or woman must be permanently obsequious, or to submit to the narrow compulsions of identifying himself and his interests with those of the social class into which he had been born? Theotokas sought a social system that would allow the unique human being the greatest allowable freedom within confines he considered basically creative, such as culture, language, and history, rather than the stultifying and inhibiting barriers of chauvinism and class loyalties.

Industrialization was a fact that need not signal a return to political and economic despotism or its concomitant, social struggle. Industrial progress *could* lead in the direction of a freer society. Though he mourned the passing of the craftsman and of his psychologically fulfilling way of life, Theotokas accepted the inevitable industrialization of Greece as a step toward the creation of a free society that would allow "the uninhibited flowering" of every human being.

The new world that had emerged from the war was to be one dominated by what Theotokas would call supernations that maintained a foothold in Europe but were not of it. The world that dawned after the nightmare of Occupation was the world he had worried about since his early manhood. There was one significant difference, however; in the United States, which assumed the one position, the Roosevelt New Deal had shackled the laissez-faire character of capitalism and imposed on it the restraints and safeguards necessary for social welfare. The Soviet Union, that other "nation-continent," however, did not seem to have changed its position significantly on personal freedoms, and as long as Stalin was to remain in power, the liberal Constitution of 1936 would continue to be a utopian document unrelated to the everyday life of the Soviet citizen.

Europe, Theotokas believed, had lost the century and would probably be unable to confront its problems with the resolve necessary to subordinate the separate national interests and traditions into a federation he thought necessary. Besides this, the era of the European genius able to synthesize a great vision in his art seemed to be over, and the great validity and power of postwar European literature and thought lay in its ability to describe its own anxiety, bitterness, and despair. A united Europe would be a superpower again, a "continent-nation" like

the U.S.S.R. and the U.S.A., but its interest in federation seemed
to be minimal and doomed to failure. The battle, therefore, was
between Russia, which used modern science and technology
but rejected Western values, and America, which had absorbed
both to create a powerful and unique state. Frightful as the
cost of war between these two megapowers would be, Theotokas
firmly believed that the victory of Russia would be a disastrous
backward step for mankind, while that of America would merely
be a continuation of the culture and civilization he loved so
much. "A victory for Russia would mean that the Persians had
won at Marathon," he was to say.

His trip to the United States emphasized three insights he
had always had. In the first place, he felt more than ever that
science, if used properly, could guarantee life and comfort
for everyone. This view was not darkened yet by a personal
loss that would remind him of the importance of religion and
the nonrational. In the second place, in confronting the vastness,
the power, and the efficiency of America, he concluded that the
separate nation-state, as Europe had developed it, was an obstacle for the better life of man. Finally, he found inescapable
the conclusion that what was needed was a worldwide economic
organization that would regulate trade but whose decisions
would be more binding than those of the United Nations or of
the League of Nations in the past. As far as the development of
governmental organizations was concerned, feudalism was superseded by the nation-state, in turn rendered obsolete by the con-
tinent state, and superseded, ultimately, by what Theotokas
called the "Ecumenical State."

Europe was clearly in the same position with respect to the
megapowers that emerged after World War II as was Greece,
important only as a pawn is important, the passive receiver of
decisions crucial to its future that are reached elsewhere, with
interests other than its own kept foremost. As it was in the
interests of Greece at the end of the 1920s to join in a Balkan
Federation, so it would be in the interests of the European
nations to join in a United States of Europe. It was the only way
progress would be achieved, and Theotokas defined progress as
that trend "that respects the freedom of the individual and
promises an increase in the standard of living of the mass"; these

would be achieved only by "the union of as many states as possible."

It is not often that the American shores have seen a foreigner as careful of his generalizations as Theotokas and, despite his more than ordinary intellectual preparation for the trip, as willing to be surprised. How could he presume to understand the American character, Theotokas wondered with characteristic caution, when even the Greek character perplexed and baffled him? In *Essay on America* Theotokas provided his reader with a generous European view of a unique and troubling reality he knew no one would ever be able to fathom completely.

In Europe, he generalized, people defined themselves as a nation by their common past; the people of the United States, on the contrary, defined themselves by their common future. As distinct from many national traditions in Europe, organized religions in the United States, because they were not established, had rarely—and never officially—been allied with reactionary forces; because of the pluralistic nature of American society, they maintained a formally impartial role in political life. Moreover, the political parties were not defined in ideological terms, as they frequently were in Europe, but in emotional and historical terms, of which Theotokas approved, since this definition allowed for flexibility in political platforms that doctrinal consistency would not permit. He advocated the instinct for federation, aware that this was the path Europe must follow eventually, but he was also fascinated by the national willingness to absorb contrarieties. For a man like Theotokas, who mourned the dissension the civil war had created among his countrymen, the sight of the statues of Jefferson Davis and Robert E. Lee in the Capitol were reminders that the wounds of the postwar social conflict in Greece would not be fully healed until the Greek State honored its recent opponents in a similar way.

Theotokas's trip to the Soviet Union in 1963, though not as interesting nor as informative as his confrontation with America, nevertheless provided him with some valuable questions. He uncovered, for example, the world of the petite bourgeoisie in what he had thought to be a classless society, and he was made aware of the identity they had gained by going to their clubs and of their joy when they moved into apartments of their own. He was surprised, moreover, by the attraction the drama of Chekhov had for the young; if *Uncle Vanya* and *The Cherry Orchard* spoke to the Soviet young and had a resonance in their deepest selves, they, too, must have felt the psychological weariness and the sadness of which Chekhov wrote. If this were true, the emphasis on rationalism, scientific progress, and industrialization had not created the new Soviet man for whom the doors to the nonrational were permanently sealed.

His trip to Russia convinced him that the U.S.S.R. would never be able to match America in economic power and efficiency, certainly not without the continuation of dictatorship. But he saw a certain similarity in the two supernations: they were large, federated states where men could rise to positions of power regardless of their nationalities: Stalin, Theotokas noted, was a Georgian; Khrushchev, a Ukrainian; and Mikoyan, an Armenian.

IV   Problems of Our Time

His travels to America and the Soviet Union showed Theotokas some aspects of the future, but as a Greek his discoveries would have no meaning unless he tried to understand his own countrymen. *Problems of Our Time* (1956) is a fine collection of six essays in which Greece and the Greek are subjected to a closer than usual scrutiny.[5] In three essays in particular, in which Theotokas studies "The Greek Writer," "Political Life," and "The Worldly Life as a Social Phenomenon," he provides insights into the character of his countrymen and their society that are valuable because they are candid revelations, from the inside, of factors that a number of impartial observers have not noticed.

The Greek writers, according to Theotokas, are people in search of an identity as well as an audience. Classifications like "professional" and "amateur" are meaningless, since only a few authors have been able to support themselves by their writing. They cannot be defined by their reading public, since such a public is nonexistent, mainly—according to Theotokas—because of the lack of a substratum of serious education enabling the readers to appreciate quality. As a result the writer is solitary. He is often suspicious of plots by dark powers—"cliques organ-

ized to choke off his expression"—and believes himself opposed
as often by his own colleagues as by a press and a state that
are indifferent to his achievements. "In this phantasy world
that has overflowed beyond measure, the solitary writer sees
himself as a neglected genius and finds his consolation in self-
admiration, in ego-worship." Frequently, in order to feel important and to provide himself with a ready audience, the writer
goes to ideological extremes, losing his identity in a political
orientation that strips him of whatever valuable insights his
uniqueness has provided him with. Recent literary history had
provided Theotokas with numerous examples of men and women
who had permitted their political stands to disorient the deeper
coherence of their art.

The writers Theotokas considered important were those who
remained true to themselves, accepting the fact—or the possibility—that they would never gain fame or money, and expressing themselves without intimidation and fear. This, he reminded
the reader, was what "Kostis Palamas was to high-school and
university boys for half a century, during national catastrophes,
mass uprootings, and civil wars." No matter what had happened
in and to Greece, the youth "knew that somewhere there was a
solitary, unbending man considering freely the issues of the
spirit, of life, and of the country, a man who did not fear to
speak the language of truth."

Greek political life, Theotokas concluded after a lifetime of
observation and an attempt in 1956 to win the parliamentary
seat for Chios, would probably never be stripped of its element
of show business, bombastic issues like "historic mission" and
"messianic personalities," its Machiavellis, its Hamlets, its turn-
coats, its cynics, its buffoons. Unlike the president of the
Swiss Confederation, who sat next to a friend of Theotokas on
a bus one day, the usual Greek politician was treated differently
from the ordinary citizen, given first-class accommodations wher-
ever he went, depended upon for services that, in another
country, would be undertaken by an appropriate and efficient
government bureau. The psychology of the Greek politician,
Theotokas remarked, was similar to that of the Greek actor, who,
as soon as he attained some sort of fame, immediately established
his own theater and placed his name in a prominent position on

the marquee. The actor could easily begin a group with others who were his equals, a troupe that would last longer and present a more varied program, but there would always be the fear that he would not stand out individually. "We have, therefore, a great number of unsuccessful theaters," he maintained, and political parties, among which politicians circulate because of pique, ambition, or loyalty to a particular leader. Some say that the system was to blame for this, but Theotokas claimed that there was no system. "The method of electing deputies has changed ten times in my generation and the language of the readers in grammar school has changed as often." The Greeks themselves were to blame, he concluded, and he called on them to "know themselves," to "leave the fog of words and see [themselves] as [they] really are."

The changes Greece was undergoing in the decade immediately following the end of the civil war were obvious to a man like Theotokas, who had always evinced an interest in his society. Despite the incremental but slow rate of growth, Greece was beginning to exhibit an affluence never before witnessed and an important change of social orientation. Social parties, for example, a subject to which Theotokas devoted a highly interesting essay, revealed that the French- or Viennese-influenced salons were institutions of the prewar past. It had become "the Anglo-Saxon cocktail party" and the dinner with small tables that dispersed the guests and scattered the conversations. These developments he considered as products of industrial civilization. There were now many guests—more, certainly, than any one table, no matter how large, could accommodate—who were often mobile and did not need to be served in static positions; this resulted in a rationalized organization and an efficient use of time—the hallmarks of industrial thought. Contrary to the customs of old Athenian society, the time to arrive and to leave were clearly indicated on the invitation, which did away with "the tiresome Greek habit" of pressing the guests to stay longer. In fact, he continued, one rarely saw one's host at a cocktail party, and in order to be heard over the roar of nearby conversationalists, one had to shout. Because the position of the guest was not fixed for the entire evening by the host, the guest was free to cruise about in a temporary social world without rigid hierarchies. The important fact about these parties was that, though business matters might not definitively be decided there, they were all, and almost exclusively, involved with business concerns. This overwhelming preoccupation with business could be disguised, however, because of the mixed nature of the gathering, and the many clusters of conversationalists allowed for a modification in the public nature of the gathering.

The insights Theotokas made into postwar Greece were among the few contributions by Greeks to a field that was dominated by social scientists from abroad who approached Greek society with tools gained in foreign—usually Anglo-American—universities. Most of these students had concentrated, until that time, on village and rural life, but an increasing number were now initiating studies in the social behavior and political organization of the urban Greek. These studies were valuable, certainly, but most of them were characterized by an objectivity that viewed the relationship between one Greek and another and between the citizen and his state in terms that were rarely flattering, while at the same time assuming that the standards—that is, the individual and social behavior common to their own nations—by which Greek society was being judged were not vulnerable to the same criticism.

Without the contributions of Theotokas to this literature, one would suspect the Greek novelists of dealing with a totally different subject matter from that treated by the social scientists from abroad. Though he was certainly not trained in sociology or anthropology, Theotokas was an astute and careful observer of a scene he knew more intimately and more profoundly than the foreign students who have written on Greek society.

Objectivity is a virtue more wished for than attained, and the observations of someone like Theotokas, precisely because they emerge from a deep awareness of the Greek past and a perpetual sense of ambivalence and ambiguity that is the residue of every humanist's training, are more convincing than the analyses of scholars whose attachment to Greece is only peripheral. It is a pity that others of his generation did not reveal the same interest in the society of which they formed an integral part: they were interested solely in documenting it, however, and not in theorizing about it.

V *Man and The Divine*

The death of Nausicaa in 1959 (after a marriage of eleven years) forced Theotokas into a spiritual crisis he might not have otherwise undergone at that point; it became increasingly evident to a careful reader of his work, however, that the positions of his youth, often characterized as "rationalist" and "Cartesian," were less and less satisfying to him as he matured. The death of his beloved wife, and the death eight years earlier, in 1951, of his respected father, were merely facts that made unavoidable the distressing tendency of human existence to confound the mind of a man of good will.

The human mind is an instrument that is frustrated unless it can find the reason for things and the logic in history, but the why and the how of human existence are ultimately incomprehensible. The human intellect cannot grasp the purpose of its being in time and cannot understand the reason for the "uninhibited flowering of its individuality within the reality of flesh and spirit"; it cannot, therefore, fulfill its reasons for existence. To reflect truly the structure of the universe that surrounds man, to be an accurate microcosm of the reality in which the human personality in its freedom is to "flower uninhibitedly," it must bear within it a respect for the irrational, an awe for the inexplicable, and an openness to the divine, which in most cultures had been likened to foolishness and madness.

We shall see this clearly in chapter 7 when Theotokas begins to treat "the principle of human madness" in *The Sacred Road*, the first part of *Invalids and Wayfarers,* a phrase he abandoned when, in the second volume, he fully illustrated it within the actions of characters who embody human ambiguity and confusion. We have seen the dark complexity of the impingement of the divine on human lives emerging as one of the leading themes of his dramas; and this preoccupation with the relationship of man and God, or, perhaps, more accurately, the need to find the source and the explanation for evil in human affairs, became manifest in the notes and articles of a religious nature that he published with greater frequency as the decade of the 1950s advanced.

There is something in man—not in the Greek alone—as man

that harms and distorts his greatest hopes, a principle of corruption in human affairs that cannot be explained by using the principles of scientific humanism. The crisis in which Theotokas found himself was relentless, for he was a man who believed both in man's promise as well as in his fatal corruption. In this spiritual dilemma, perhaps unusual for a Greek thinker in contemporary times, Theotokas turned to the Orthodox church for guidance and found it unprepared.

Greek Orthodoxy, for historical reasons, had been confounded with the nationalist aspirations of the modern Greek to the point where most Greeks—and this applied to the religious as well—were unable to distinguish between Orthodoxy and Hellenism. Theotokas himself was occasionally capable of confusing the two, but he at least was conscious of the distinction.

Since the church had been satisfied to cultivate the easy marriage between Hellenism and Christianity, issues whose identification depended upon a clear awareness of the essential differences between religion and nationality were not being faced. These were not exclusively social issues but had much to do with the relationship between man and God. The fact that Greek Orthodoxy, because of the four centuries of Turkish subjugation, had not undergone a doctrinal challenge and a reformation meant that many moral, philosophic, and theological problems had not been confronted. What, for example, were the positions of the church on the scientific, technological, and political developments in the past century?

The church and its representatives, Theotokas discovered to his dismay, had not kept pace with the society they were to serve. Aside from its physical presence, the only role the church seemed to fulfill in Greek life was that of a legal entity as the established religion of the Greek state. If this venerable institution, whose history stretched back almost two millenia, appeared to have little to offer a man like Theotokas, what could it say to someone who did not feel ties of loyalty to it at all? Beyond the genuine interest Theotokas had begun to develop in the religious orientation to life, there was—and perhaps this was the motivating force behind his interest—the residue of loyalty to the Orthodox church Theotokas felt because of his family background. As a result of this loyalty, the rationalist

Theotokas could not be certain that the church had little to offer him until he had tested these insights himself.

And he seemed to be virtually on his own. Aside from Alexander Papadiamandis, there appeared to be no important Greek men of letters in the past who could be identified with a religious orientation, and there were certainly no theologians or intellectuals in the Orthodox Greek world who could have provided an ideological alternative to the Western rationalism that had so clearly proved inadequate. There were the contemporary Russian thinkers, of course, but aside from Nikolai Berdyaev we cannot be certain he had read any. The only answer to the various religious questions that emerged in his life, and it was the solution posed in most of his work for the theater, was the total abandonment of the secular world and its necessary compromises; that is, the solution was the monastic one. It appears, therefore, that Theotokas was unable to improve upon the answers the Orthodox church had given many centuries before the emergence of the modern problems that he had thought Orthodoxy was unable to confront in a relevant manner. Perhaps there were no modern answers to the questions of modern man but merely the same old answers that were valid from time immemorial.

Because of the intellectual implications of this possibility, Theotokas traveled in 1960 to the Holy Land, where he visited a number of monasteries, including Saint Catherine's on Mount Sinai, and later went to the monastic republic of Mount Athos.

The trip to Mount Sinai convinced him that the modern Greek had allowed himself to forget much of his past by considering only the West as a legitimate source of interest and influence. George Theotokas was, after all, a leading member of the Generation of the Thirties, a group of men and women who wanted to keep pace with European developments. The attitudes of someone like Fotis Kontoglou were antithetical to the deepest aspirations of this group. Yet, in the taxicab of Mr. Pericles—another Asia Minor refugee—the rationalist Theotokas traveled through the fierce Old Testament landscape of the Sinai Peninsula, in the company of three Greek priests who sang hymns to Catherine and her monastery. "How can I deny it, my fathers," he thought, "that—yes—we have given too much significance to the pretty words of the doubters and have forgotten the essentials."

This, the "oriental" part of him, he felt, was an inalienable part of the Greek tradition, too, an unexploited asset for the Greek artist who had devoted so much of himself to "the ordinary and exhausted" sources that had at one time inspired him. This Greek artist, Theotokas believed, should travel to Mount Sinai and test himself and his powers. This, of course, was an instance of the constant Greek preoccupation with Greekness. The East was another aspect of the Greek spirit, but the Greek artist's lack of interest in this important part of his racial past had seriously harmed his culture, atrophied it, so that it was in danger of becoming merely Western. We are reminded of the issue of Greekness that reemerged in the 1930s as a result of the commemorative volume of Pericles Yiannopoulos's works in *Nea Grammata,* and we find unresolved the same concern in rescuing seemingly lost fragments of a racial totality. "Hellenism" Theotokas wrote, "appears to us at times like an old, vast and—in many places—ruined mansion, full of crypts, secret cellars, and casks that have remained sealed for centuries. Whenever we happen to open them, we are dazzled by the treasures we possess and of which we are ignorant."[6]

But this "crypt," because of the steady decline of the Greek monastic population in the monastery of Saint Catherine's, might soon be forever lost to the "ruined mansion of Hellenism," as was the Patriarchate of Antioch.

The trip to Mount Athos allowed him a more direct confrontation with current Orthodox thought. Aside from viewing the Byzantine iconography of men like Panselinos, he met learned monks like Paul, a surgeon who had studied in Athens and Paris and had served with the Turkish army in the First World War and with the Greek army during the Asia Minor Disaster; or like Father Abakoum, from whom he learned about the mystical quietism of the Hesychasts and the concept of "uncreated light" that was to play such a role in *Invalids and Wayfarers*; or like Father Gerasimos, an important poet, hymnographer, and intellectual who, Theotokas was certain, had "seen" the "uncreated light"; or, finally, like Father Theoklitos, whose *Between Heaven and Earth,* despite what Theotokas considered its rigid and austere character, had much to teach the inquiring younger intellectuals "who are not indifferent to the problem of faith."

All in all, Theotokas's stay on the Holy Mountain gave him much to consider about the lack of faith, the anxieties, and the "symptoms of metaphysical agony" characterizing the century that began in what he described as "that nightmarish year" of 1914. He left Mount Athos refreshed but not reoriented; he was better prepared to confront the most recent consequences of the "1914 nightmare," but without the *personal* certitude that would have resulted from a religious conversion, which, perhaps, he might have sought. There, on Mount Athos, he had seen an answer, the monastic answer, one in keeping with the ancient and richly panoplied tradition of Orthodox mysticism and worldly rejection, but it had not fully satisfied him. If it had, he would have stayed there, like the other educated and worldly men whom he had met and talked to on Mount Athos.

Theotokas was too much the secular intellectual to withdraw into a changeless world of prayer and meditation, too much the citizen of the City of Man to be fully satisfied with the contemplation of the City of God. The monastic answer may have addressed itself directly and eloquently to the question Theotokas had formulated, but he was not personally prepared to accept its uncompromising finality. Though the religious quest Theotokas had embarked on could not provide him with a personal certitude, it had given him a profound and age-old insight that could not but be valuable to him as a novelist.

As he was leaving the peninsula, an American satellite circled in the heavens above him. It made him experience a strange sense of consolation that Mount Athos remained the repository of Christian idealism in an onrushing world of material and technological progress.

It was as a result of these chastening experiences—the decade of war, occupation, famine and civil strife, as well as the facts of personal loss—that the attitudes of Theotokas mellowed and deepened. His awareness of the dark side of life added a rich complexity to his fiction, which it may have lacked before. Where previously his commentary on history, politics, and society may have been perceptive and convincing, they were to be characterized by profundity and wisdom in what were to be the last few years of his life.

CHAPTER 7

Invalids and Wayfarers

*I*NVALIDS *and Wayfarers* (1964), the novel that was for the mature Theotokas the counterpart to his earlier novel, *Argo*, was like the first major effort a limited artistic success. The risk of failure is higher in the execution of a novel whose meaning cannot be expressed within the confines of a single volume but which requires two or more major parts for its realization. The desire to make a major statement about the human experience within historical time in a multivolume work is fraught with aesthetic dangers, as many unreadable and unread novel cycles attest. Most of the writers who have been tempted by the *roman fleuve* have emerged chilled and waterlogged from the plunge. Those who are considered successful are praised more for some novels in the cycle than for others, which are rarely if ever read. Many impressive ships have run aground on novel-rivers whose sources of inspiration have run dry. Sartre's *Roads of Freedom* has yet to find its way home with a fourth and concluding volume, while *The Alexandrian Quartet* of Lawrence Durrell, the *Dance to the Music of Time* cycle of Anthony Powell, and the *Strangers and Brothers* cycle of C. P. Snow, whether complete at this time of writing (1974) or not, are of arguable aesthetic value.

Invalids and Wayfarers, like *Argo* before it, was planned in two stages and executed in two volumes; in each novel, the first book reveals a more elegant architecture and a more convincing characterization than the concluding book. The reason for this, as far as *Invalids and Wayfarers* is concerned, can only be that the writer's interest in his subject matter changed in the interval of execution from the surface and chronological portrayal of historical events in the manner of an accomplished muralist-narrator to the profound questioning of motive and responsibility in human events characteristic of the moralist and of the psychological novelist. As far as the interest of Theotokas is concerned, both major works of fiction reveal a conscious interposition of distance between the reader and the action as the novels progress. In *Argo* the focus shifts from the exhilarating narrative drive of political involvement to the more personal and psychological preoccupations of the youthful characters, whereas in *Invalids and Wayfarers* the story progresses from the skillful chronological narration of Greece's entry into the Second World War to the painstaking analysis of the vulnerability and guilt of human beings immersed in the whirlpool of history.

I *Volume One:* The Sacred Road

The Sacred Road, the first volume of *Invalids and Wayfarers,* was published in 1950 when Theotokas was forty-four years old. The second volume, bearing the title of the entire work (and almost twice the length of *The Sacred Road*) appeared in 1964 when he was fifty-eight. Since the first volume was published immediately after a decade of war, occupation, famine, resistance, liberation, and civil wars, the experiences of that brutal decade were not memories to Theotokas but immediate and raw facts. It is conceivable, then, and Theotokas admits as much, that he was unable to see in 1950 that *The Sacred Road* was not a complete artistic statement but an introduction to a much broader canvas: the decade that began in triumph, passed through the inferno of subjugation, privation, and civil strife, and ended in the relative calm of reconstruction.

The two major personages of *The Sacred Road* are Kyriakos Kostakareas, an enlisted man intimidated by his mother and two unmarried sisters and, as a result, frightened of women; and Marinos Velis, a capable and idealistic officer who is the lover of Theano Galati, a leading tragedienne of the Athens stage. Both are literary men, though Kyriakos has not attained the relative stature of Marinos. The events of the war's later stages— from the expulsion of the Italian armies from Greek soil to the entry of the Germans into Athens—are by and large chronicled through the alternating points of view of the two men. There are recourses to the unlimited omniscient narrator—the least convincing segments of the book—when Theotokas wants to describe genuine historical moments and characters like King George II, Prime Minister Koryzis, and various British generals.

It is Kyriakos, however, who is the central character of *The Sacred Road,* since it is he who knows all of the important characters and who is changed by the events of the novel. Besides this, he is a far more interesting figure than the bland Marinos, who is full of vague philosophic statements and an unrelenting idealism. The most interesting aspect to Marinos is his relationship with Theano. Perhaps the problem is that he appears in the novel fully developed as a character, though unclear in outline, and has little or no further definition to attain as a result of the fictional events.

Kyriakos, on the contrary, appears as a man with much potential, and the war experience he is undergoing will provide him, we are led to believe, with all of the requisite possibilities for personal growth. When we first meet him he feels himself to be a failure, cowed by people and events, timid, and envious of his friends' achievements, confidence, and women. It is no accident that he is obsessed by both Theano and Marietta, the attractive wife of his good friend, Thrasyvoulos Drakos, desiring them not simply as lovers but as symbols of masculine freedom from his own oppressive women at home, proofs, in other words, of sexual mastery and social achievement.

With the defeat of the Greek and Allied forces and their retreat to the capital, Kyriakos is paradoxically liberated in the chaos that follows. There no longer exists a social order, at least not until the Germans enter Athens. He rapes Amalia, a waitress of dubious character and—in a rare moment of heedlessness—hangs the forbidden Greek flag from his balcony as a gesture of contempt toward the German invaders who will soon raise their own flag of conquest on the Acropolis.

Of all the characters in *The Sacred Road,* only Kyriakos Kostakareas changes and develops through the novel's action, while Marinos Velis, whose personal complexity should have made him a three-dimensional character, remains a thoughtful man who merely incorporates within himself the experiences gained from his participation in the last-ditch battle beyond the Greek borders and the slow retreat back to Athens. He does not, however, change in any appreciable way.

Minor characters are not expected to develop or change. As long as they are convincing, it is enough for them to be two-dimensional. Frixos Avgoustis, the adventurer who exists only as a break from the unremitting reality of the narrative events, need be, for example, no more than caricature, a Euripides Pendozalis dragged into the decade of the 1940s. Maleas, a Communist imprisoned by the Metaxas dictatorship in the jails of Acronauplion, is no more than a name, while Captain Paradeisis, Marinos's commanding officer, provides a lovely but hurried sketch of a peaceable man in time of war. Douglas MacDougall, a Scots sergeant, is like Avgoustis, a caricature of the Highlander in Greece, while Theano Galati is only an aura of beauty, not a real and convincing woman. Even Marinos addresses her at one point as his "goddess."

The vital and interesting Thrasyvoulos Drakos remains what he is at the beginning, a politically oriented intellectual who views the Germans as passing conquerors and sees the major threat to Greece in Communists like Maleas, a friend of Kyriakos. It is Drakos who explicitly states these ideas in the interregnum of peace before the full brunt of the German Occupation. When he, his wife, and Kyriakos go to a taverna, they are insulted by a waiter who considers them representatives of a bourgeois Greece now about to perish. "Isn't it enough that you sent us to die for your interests? Your State has collapsed. It's someone else's turn now." This comment excites Thrasyvoulos enough to make him express his fears of a struggle between Right and Left. "We must take the situation in our hands, otherwise they will take it. Communism will take it." When Marietta, in anguish, asks, "What do you mean by we and they. . . ? Aren't we one [people]? Aren't we one nation, one great family, united in misfortune, like orphaned brothers and sisters?" The answer is clear and remorseless.

They are the dissolution of everything, decomposition, chaos, death. We stand for the simple, the positive, the honorable. That is, the middle class, the only real ruling class of Greece, the thousands of hard-working people who educate themselves, labor, create, and constantly spur the progress of the country. We were responsible for

the Revolution of 1821, we organized the State and all of our civilization, we supported the great policies of Eleftherios Venizelos. We
should again take command and save the nation. Otherwise, Kyriakos's friend, Maleas, will take it.[1]

This sounds a major historical chord in the novel, and it is
symptomatic, perhaps, that it is neither Kyriakos nor Marinos
who expresses it. Though Athens is now defenseless and defeated and though all the major characters of the novel are
waiting for the new order to be imposed on them by the current
conqueror, the reader is informed that political and social issues
vital to the volume he has been reading are actually peripheral
to the author's concerns. What those concerns are, because of
the fourteen years separating the first from the second volume,
seem not to be clear to Theotokas himself.

The architectural elegance, the clarity of action, and the narrative power that sustain *The Sacred Road* to the end prove
to be qualities that are tangential and indirect, not organically
tied to the major theme, which has not been identified as yet.
Fixed as the reader is on the action of the first volume, he can
see only that Kyriakos has made his decision to resist the
invader before Baron von Hertemberg blares his greeting to
the Führer over the radio station of Athens and the German
flag flutters from the Acropolis. When the telephone rings and
a recently freed Maleas, the Communist friend of the protagonist, tells Kyriakos that he has been in Athens since the previous
day, the reader knows that the heretofore undecided central
character is prepared to make a commitment that will change
his life.

Excepting, therefore, the internal struggle of Kyriakos to
liberate himself from the psychosexual bonds that his society
and civilization have imposed on him, only one fictional conflict remains in *The Sacred Road* and that is external, the national
struggle of the Greeks against the invaders. Every other possibility for conflict is arrested at the rudimentary stage to be
developed after the German Occupation has become a fact.
The Sacred Road, as was obvious to some of Theotokas's readers,
was not an independent novel but an introduction, a "direction"
that the subsequent book had to take.

The ideas explicitly stated in it by the characters are unimportant because they are lost, subdued in the vast epic of the battles between the Greeks and the Axis powers. Only the repeated insights of Kyriakos on the role of madness in human affairs promises the reader an interpretation of man in the world and in history that, he is led to believe, will bear fruit in the second volume.[2]

Kyriakos is thus the central hero: because his actions and thoughts open and close *The Sacred Road*, because he is the personage all the others know in common, and because he moves from a static position of noncommitment to active engagement. His psyche, at this juncture, appears to be the battleground of the converging forces in the novel. With the destruction of the Greek state and the ensuing disorder, and with the substitution by the Germans of the morality of force for whatever legal and moral order may have existed under the Metaxas government, Kyriakos is free to act in a way that will help him discover and create his own values.

Theotokas could go no further in 1950 than he did. The civil war was still fresh and Kyriakos's stance was much too important and emotionally weighted for the writer to see it dispassionately. After all, Kyriakos might have become another Communist like Damianos Frantzis. Into what troubled waters would that have taken Theotokas? The political climate of the 1950s could never be mistaken as being similar to that of the 1930s; his portrait of Frantzis may have been the proof of a young novelist's interest in ideas, but a fuller treatment of Maleas might have been interpreted in the post–civil war decade as a dangerous trafficking in "antinational" ideas by his peers of the Center and Right and as insidious defamation by writers of the extreme Left, who would have been forbidden, by the political realities of the time, from criticizing his work on ideological grounds.

"The fact was," Theotokas writes in the prologue to the second edition, "that even I did not know, did not 'see' anything further in the life of my characters after the entry of the German army into Athens."[3] It was merely a "block" attributable to the nearness—both historical and psychological—of the decade's horrors, and one common not only to authors whose ambition leads them to subject matter impossible to deal with in one volume but to artists attracted to material that partakes of the documentary, the journalistic, and the contemporary. The ephemeral, which entices the artist to grapple with issues in the foreground of his preoccupations, abandons him at the precise moment his achievement overtakes it. He finds himself in a position of stasis, the deep sources of his unconscious unengaged, like a hunter who has overtaken and lost his prey.

II *Volume Two*: Invalids and Wayfarers

As in *Argo*, the reader experiences in Volume Two an unmistakable distance between himself and events as the novelist retreats from narrative to reflection. It is not by chance that the second part of *Invalids and Wayfarers* begins with "The Archives of the Monk Timotheos," the religious name taken by Marinos Velis when he gave up secular life to take holy orders. This should remind us of the "Notebook of Lambros Christides," placed between the two parts of *Argo* and termed "Intermedio." As in *Argo*, the aesthetic expectations as developed in the first part are changed. In *Argo*, as we noted, the two important characters, Damianos Frantzis and Pavlos Skinas, were emptied of interest and reality and pushed away from the center of action. In *Invalids and Wayfarers* something less drastic is done. Only Kyriakos is pushed aside, while Marinos emerges, not as a leading fictional character but as the novelist's persona, the intellect through whom Theotokas sees the action. The action that he sees, however, has already taken place. It is a *review* of action frozen in the past, action in which, by the very nature of his war service, Marinos was barred from participating. As a result, he, too, is emptied of interest for us, his mind becoming only the loophole through which we see the actions of characters either previously unknown to us or possessing less significance than they did in *The Sacred Road*.

The major character in the second volume is Theano Galati, and the major story line is her collaboration with the German authorities during the Occupation, motivated first by her decision to save the lives of Greeks (notably Kyriakos Kostakareas) imprisoned by the S.S. and ultimately by her love for

Ernst Hillebrand, an S.S. officer who is aide to Baron von Hertemberg. For this collaboration she is executed by the EAM at
a kangaroo court during the December battles.

Volume two[4] tells this story through the technique of mul-
tiple narrators. Marinos, while narrating his wartime experiences,
reveals his slow comprehension of the actions and the death
of the woman he loves and documents his decision to go to
Mount Athos. Theano, in a series of letters that become, in
effect, a personal journal, outlines her involvement with, and
confesses her love for, Hillebrand. In a deposition given to
"The Foundation for the Study of Modern Greek History," an
actor met briefly in *The Sacred Road* relates his personal encounter with the EAM, his meeting with Theano at the "Phoe-
bus" cinema in Peristeri, the events of the trial—chaired by
Maleas, who reveals Hillebrand's role in the transportation of
the Salonika Jews to the concentration camps—and her execution. In the fourth segment of "The Archives," Kyriakos, a minor
character by now, explains his conversion to the EAM cause
and his personal view of Theano's trial.

This specific historical event[5] provides the factual basis for a
highly complex treatment of the relativity of history. "The Survivors" gives us two more interpretations of Theano's affair
with Hillebrand, which are interesting because they at first
appear to contradict each other. One states that Hillebrand
almost treasonously passed to Theano certain papers that got
into the hands of the British intelligence network and thus
saved a warehouse full of explosives from the EAM, whereas
the other, held by Theano's cousin, a general, supports the view
that the papers were passed to the Royalists and the British but
holds that by the time the Royalists got to the warehouse the
explosives were gone, probably taken by the EAM. The Royalist
officer does not seem to consider the possibility that the British
got to the warehouse and took the explosives without informing their Greek allies.

The major fictional event of this second volume, therefore,
is the love and death of Theano Galati. The fates of Marinos
Velis and Kyriakos Kostakareas are pushed into the background.
The problems caused by this change in direction are serious and
not solely from a narrow technical perspective. Not only does

Theotokas go from narration to reflection (which explains the distance between reader and fictional events), but he is compelled, as a novelist, to place Marinos in dramatic and historical situations that were not direct experiences of his own. This results in a number of scenes without particular immediacy, like the generalized and journalistic view of the Battle of El Alamein. Theotokas needed to remove Marinos from Athens in order to leave Theano lonely and unprotected, ready for an affair with Hillebrand, but he could not place him in the partisan camps since this would have demanded from him, not only a specific ideological commitment, an important consideration, but also references to a way of life about which he could, again, have no firsthand knowledge.

The fictional value of Marinos Velis, however, is his ideological freedom. He was described in *The Sacred Road* as an ideologue. But how can he be an ideologue without a definite ideological position? What Theotokas meant by this, one supposes, is that Marinos was characterized by an all-absorbing interest in political and social thought but was unable or unwilling to limit his actions and insights to the narrow and often restricting demands of a theory, whose great value and mortal weakness is that it must be *consistent*.

The fictional problem created by this stance is that life itself, with distressing regularity, compels men and women to make commitments they would rather avoid. Marinos's sojourn in the Middle East, his participation in the Desert War, his arrival in Athens after the December events, and his decision to enter the monastery seem to be too convenient for the novelist, since they enable him to keep Marinos ideologically free until the novel's end. But how can one remain ideologically free in the monastic life? Somehow, Marinos manages to do this. Having accepted the necessity to pray and expiate the guilt he feels because of his abandonment of Theano, he leaves the monastery when he feels ready to do so: when the world has settled down, when order has been reestablished.

Marinos Velis is a thinker, not a doer. Despite his monastic vocation, he seems to have drifted out of his religious commitment, allowing himself to follow the historical flow as he drifted beyond the point where the commitment he and Theano had

toward each other was meaningful. Certainly, it served Theotokas's purposes to have Marinos remain ideologically free,
uncommitted to any specific political philosophy, but he seems
to have retained this freedom at the price of meshing with his
personal history. In Christian terms, he might be considered a
sinner by omission rather than by commission. He has sinned
because he has not acted deeply or committed himself, because
he guarded his freedom too much.

Kyriakos Kostakareas, however, "sins," in other words, goes
wrong, because he commits himself to the EAM, meshes with
historical reality, and accepts a world view; then, alienated by
it but unwilling to capitulate totally by signing a recantation of
his views, he gradually develops the impression that history has
tricked him. For a brief moment he has accepted the Procrustean bed of Maleas's ideology, uplifted by his sense of solidarity with his people in their struggle against the Germans; but
then, with the defeat of EAM comes doubt, or doubt comes
independently of defeat. Since he has committed himself by
choosing sides in history, he—unlike Marinos—has to confess his
change formally. His compromise with the status quo, his lack
of interest in issues and ideologies, is a defeat that brings him
back full circle to what he was.

No one is happy in this world of "invalids and wayfarers." In
the Greek Orthodox tradition invalids and wayfarers are exempted from the rigid canonical demands of the strict fast. They
do not lose Grace, even though they cannot follow all the rules:
they are not strong, after all, and have a long way to go on
their journey.

But who are the strong? Minor characters who are killed off
stage. It is only *their* faith that is not shaken. They die, committed to their cause, unable at the end to convince the reader
of their reality. Both Maleas and Lukas Amygdalos, a soldier
holding the Christian view whom Marinos meets briefly, are
killed at the Battle of Grammos in 1949.

One might inquire as to why these two are not elevated in
importance so that their intellectual insights, the *systems* that
organized their beliefs into a coherent view of the world and
man's destiny in it, can help focus the problems Theotokas was
dealing with in *Invalids and Wayfarers*. The kind of man that

Maleas is, however, no longer interested Theotokas. He had already portrayed him in *Argo* through Damianos Frantzis and had nothing new to add to his portrait of the true believer. By this time in Theotokas's life, people like Maleas could not call forth a response from him; they are what theologians call the "invincibly ignorant," men and women so armored by rationalism and so imprisoned on the surface of life that only a "fictional miracle," what Aristotle in his *Poetics* considered a "possible" rather than a "probable" cause, could dislodge and plunge them into an existential view of life. Maleas, as we see him, could never understand Unamuno's statement in *The Tragic Sense of Life* that "if it is nothingness that awaits us, let us make an injustice of it." The only injustice Maleas can see is the historical one, about which he has long since ceased being emotional. A dedicated Communist, imprisoned many times for his beliefs, he is not about to begin undermining his position by questioning the sources of his action and the purpose of his self. He is *self-less* in his effort to bring about a new world, and Theotokas had always maintained the sacredness of the self.

Lukas Amygdalos would probably have understood the Spaniard's comment, but Theotokas was not quite prepared to commit himself to a religious interpretation of life. As we have seen, he had already manifested in his theatrical works an interest in religion during the Occupation, and this had deepened and developed during the intervening years, but *Invalids and Wayfarers,* his major postwar effort in fiction, was too complex and diffuse a work, and its writing extended over too many years, to allow Theotokas the sharp focus demanded by shorter fiction and drama. His quest for—or, perhaps, more accurately, his interest in—a theological dimension to life had emerged in his fiction only after *The Sacred Road* had been published. In the second volume we see Theotokas preoccupied by the deep recesses of the human mind, with the irrationality of emotion, with a good woman's passionate love for an enemy who is a committed Nazi, a love that is narrated through *her* viewpoint and filtered through the mind of Marinos Velis, the novel's most sympathetic character. These facts should prove that Theotokas's goal in the second volume was not the ordinary historical novelist's objective. Perhaps Lukas Amygdalos should have been a more important character than he was, but his emergence into the foreground would have obscured Kyriakos Kostakareas even more. His commitment to a religious way of life, moreover, might have emphasized more strongly Marinos's indecisiveness, and it would have threatened the reader's acceptance of the profundity and believability of his monastic vocation.

What of the other characters? Surfacing in the novel's second volume, like a menacing shark, is an important figure who supplies Theotokas with the energizer of the plot action and with a new development in his portrait gallery, a careerist no longer viewed with the delight he had shown toward Euripides Pendozalis or the understanding he had exhibited toward Pavlos Skinas. Vardekis is a new species, a man whose only desire is to survive and grow powerful. He collaborates with the Germans and works secretly with the Resistance and the Allies, desperately trying to hedge all his bets, his fertile mind never lacking justification for his actions. "He worked for the nation. If a genuine national need did not exist he would not sacrifice his person and his future in this position, this very dangerous position, he had assumed, etc. etc" (p. 264). Unlike the others, he manages to survive intact, but he has no moral or ideological baggage to carry through historical change. One wonders what place Vardekis would occupy in the moral scheme of Theotokas. Though "invalids and wayfarers" are exempted from the strict adherence to rules, some adherence is necessary. Vardekis believes in nothing but survival and power. He is cunning, whereas the others, like Theano, for whose meeting with Hillebrand Vardekis himself is responsible, are not. They are sucked down by the maelstrom. Vardekis bobs up and postwar Greece finds him with vast economic and political power. He is the scavenger of history. Perhaps, as in Coleridge's "The Ancient Mariner," God will bless him too, but since Theotokas seems not to have forgiven him, neither can the reader.

But he can forgive Frixos Avgoustis, because this fantast and liar who could have become anything in *The Sacred Road*, is not to be taken seriously. In volume two he reveals cowardice on the front line and a clear, almost clinical case of insanity. When Hollywood claims him as a writer of screenplays under the name of Felix August, the reader is as surprised as when Douglas MacDougall and Amalia surface happily married in Aberdeen as owners of a restaurant.

In this large mural of Greek life that Theotokas has painted, however, all the meaningful characters are broken by events. Ernst Hillebrand, a true believer in Hitler, wanders aimlessly after the Nazi defeat, having lost his faith in a god who had given meaning to his life. Thrasyvoulos Drakos, a partisan in EDES, feels that, despite his previous attitudes about communism, he has made the wrong decision and that he should be fighting instead in the ranks of EAM-ELAS; a little before his death in the December battles, fighting for a cause he no longer believes in (just as his friend, Kyriakos, has lost faith in his own cause) he seems to have accepted the Marxist world view. Theano has died in a dishonor from which neither her own lame justifications nor the compassion of Theotokas can quite rescue her.

Life is chaotic and the rules of morality do not always apply. Great historical events are like fevers in which people say and do things for which they must not be held too strictly accountable. Grace still operates, even though mortals—invalids and wayfarers, as they all are—are exempted from some of the less important rules.

If Theotokas himself had not written *Invalids and Wayfarers,* Theotokas—the Apollonian essayist and critic—might have been alienated by the novel's depiction of the defeat of sensitive men and women by brutal and amoral historical forces. He might have rejected the essential meaning of the novel as another example of the prevailing nihilism that had overcome the West. There is no aesthetic rule that demands that a novelist must consciously accept the world view reflected in his work, but the reader must not be given the impression that the author himself is busily "trying on" different interpretations of life in a novel that is supposed to be a commentary on life. The reader detects a conflict in Theotokas that is perhaps the most interesting and central fact of his literary career.

The surface calm of the documentarylike *Sacred Road* gives no indication of the existential anguish of the second volume, and the work as a whole does not exhibit a coherent world view but one in the process of change. This transitional process takes place within the confines of the same aesthetic statement and flaws irredeemably the reader's comprehension of the protagonist, Marinos Velis, and his view of life, which must be taken as representative of the author's at this point in his career.

It is significant that this most urbane and intellectual of Greeks would sense the profound upheaval of a religious crisis at the precise moment when his nation was beginning to develop industrially and, apparently, to settle into a social stability. The result of this conflict between mind and spirit was a confusion in value systems. *Invalids and Wayfarers* is an eloquent confession of modern man's perplexity through the fictional world he invents.

Marinos Velis, his persona, goes from one value system to another without believing in either and without renouncing his belief in one or the other. He leaves the monastery saying:

> Faith is love. A bubbling, an overflowing, a flooding of love. I love Christ and because of this believe in Him. And my love for Him . . . gives me the strength to gaze steadfastly at the world's reality and makes me feel that—whatever may happen—nothing has been lost, that there is always hope. (p. 452)

Yet, expressing his view that something is wrong with the world, he can still disagree with his abbot that "the world is lost." Why? "I do not accept this," he says because he believes "that the source can be found somewhere, that it has not gone dry." Christ, therefore, despite Marinos's love for Him, is not enough. Another source exists in the world, and it is this source that will satisfy Marinos, if and when and *where* he discovers it.

> Somewhere the source can be found, I know, I believe firmly that it exists somewhere, but it is hidden and I can't see it. Perhaps in the silence of nature or in the vast, exciting and light-bedecked cities of the Western world, perhaps in the monuments of the ancient civilizations of the East, or among the recently emerged nations, perhaps in the tropical jungles, perhaps in the lands of organized atheism; somewhere I sense it, I hear it, I long for it. (p. 454)

If he, and Theotokas, believed that no values existed, that all opinions were relative, the reader would have no qualms. After all, the relativity of values is probably the first article of the Credo of most readers today. The reader is disturbed only that Marinos does not admit this to himself, does not confess that his monastic vocation was an escape from life's complexity and its moral relativity, and that his return to the world comes about after he has attained psychic equilibrium. Did he lose this psychic balance when he learned of Theano's dishonor and death? Was the monastery just a place to hide from the necessity of committing himself to a decision, political or otherwise, about contemporary life, a retreat into a world view that, regardless of his passing psychological condition, must be viewed as either retrogressive or valid?

Marinos, the central consciousness of *Invalids and Wayfarers,* is unable to bear the weight of the novel's morality. He cannot do so because Theotokas was artistically unwilling to ·accept ethically the world with which his imagination presented him and unable to take a position that satisfied his sense of both historical and emotional truth concerning the decade of the 1940s. He is to be commended for not taking the tragic view, since it might have rounded off many of the novel's moral complexities, but he confronts the reader with a "found" world, one that on the surface reflects traditional and even Christian values yet, in its depths, contains all the horrible monsters we recognize as our everyday companions. But these were depths whose terrors Theotokas was fated to sound before his death.

A year before he died, Theotokas discovered, as a novelist, that the Christian world view was capable of providing him with more than resonant phrases, an intellectual ornamentation, a minor character or two, or an interesting perspective for viewing the personages of his fiction. He was to discover with the writing of *The Bells* that the religious orientation to life to which he was slowly adapting himself could provide a possible explanation for what would otherwise be inexplicable.

CHAPTER 8

The Combatant Again

THEOTOKAS, in the latter part of the 1950s and the early years of the 1960s began to achieve the status of an established writer whose views on most subjects were known through frequent publication and exposure. He began to identify himself with the political establishment of Greece when the wounds of the civil war began to heal and when a gradually developing mellowness on the part of the conservative Right, the party in power within the constitutional framework, began to be evident. It was only a matter of time before the Center, with its more libertarian views, would replace the Right as the government of Greece, at which point the ideas of men like Theotokas, of the group around *Epoches*,[1] and of educational reformers like Evangelos Papanoutsos would become the functioning ideas of intellectual and cultural life. Since the triumph of libertarian democracy seemed assured in time, therefore, Theotokas ran the danger of so identifying himself with the establishment that he would view every critical comment upon the status quo as a threat.

An indication of what might have happened to Theotokas if he had continued to identify himself with the Greek status quo can be seen as a result of the Formentor Conference held on the island of Corfu in the early summer of 1963, when the writer Kay Cicellis stated, in a report published in the newspaper *Vima* of May 2, 1963, that Greek writers must pay for their books to be published and that many must "exile" themselves in order to find a reading public. Why Theotokas decided to embroil himself in an issue in which he had nothing personal at stake is a mystery, though Cicellis concludes that it may have had something to do with his not wanting to show his nation's dirty linen outside the closed world of Greek life. He responded,

146

however, with a letter to the newly formed *Epoches,* of whose editorial committee he was a member, disputing both of her comments, citing the fact that there were six publishers in Athens who accepted books as commercial ventures, and stating that only Kazantzakis needed to exile himself to discover a public.

The fact is that most writers in Greece must pay to have their own works published, since the market is not great enough to warrant a fully functioning publishing industry, and this includes some of the established authors. This point was made by a number of correspondents in subsequent issues of *Epoches* beginning with George Savidis, who replied that Cicellis's news story was a Greek translation from a statement made originally in English and thus subject to misinterpretation. Besides this, Savidis named a number of novelists just achieving prominence who had great difficulty publishing their works because of the very conditions Cicellis complained about. As far as those writers who had to exile themselves were concerned, he would add to Kazantzakis, Margarita Liberaki and Nikitas Kalamais, including the "internal émigrés" like Kosmas Politis, Nikos Gatsos, and Zizis Oikonomou, though he did not indicate how their "exile" helped them to find a reading public but merely showed their alienation from Greece while remaining within the national borders.

K. Dafnis, who, in explaining the workings of the Formentor Prize, implied that one of the reasons for the controversy was perhaps the sense that a newer group of writers—men like Costas Taktsis, Vasilis Vasilikos, and Pandelis Prevelakis—whose works were about to be published abroad at that time and who were championed by Cicellis and Kimon Friar, were beginning to arouse an interest independent of support from the Greek "establishment." Friar and Cicellis, Daphnis claimed, were merely trying to explain to foreign publishers the hard life of struggling Greek writers.

There is not much that Theotokas could say to all this. Why should he defend publishing realities to which he had objected in the past, for example, in his essay on "The Greek Writer" in *Problems of our Time.* He attempted to explain the Holy Synod's condemnation of Kazantzakis, but was not convincing and withdrew from the battle.[2]

I *The Problem of Belief*

More and more Theotokas was becoming aware of a need to sound a profundity he felt within himself, a pursuit of another dimension in life that his training and his era had never allowed him to nurture. Overwhelmed all his life by the historical events and political turmoils that kept his attention permanently fixed upon the terrestrial and ephemeral, guided by a temperament intolerant of what was termed the mystical when it was merely unclear, and unsupported, finally, by an intellectual tradition within Greek Orthodoxy that was mature enough to have offered him at least one spiritual thinker of any stature, Theotokas was left to piece together a religious answer in the pages of a newspaper of the democratic center that might possibly interest a rationalist leadership which viewed the church as little more than a museum of the national traditions and its leadership as a quarrelsome group of civil servants, whose only interest seemed to be in personal advancement and the welfare of their own bureaucracies.

A series of articles published in several Christmas issues of *Vima,* reprinted in *Nea Estia,* and collected finally, under the general title of "Return to the Roots" in *Intellectual Journey,* indicates the orientation through which Theotokas was to view the problem of belief in his time. Though the era in which he had been born, educated, and grown to manhood would never permit him an easy optimism, Theotokas to this time could be considered a man whose ultimate hope for a better life for humanity lay in man's rationality. His drama was little known in his time, certainly, and the secret doubts, the frustrations, and the horrors of war, occupation, and civil strife were too often objectified and blamed on others. The principle of corruption, phrased in personal, social, and theological terms was not a usual topic in Greek literary circles, but it was this very subject that Theotokas was to introduce to the readers of *Vima* in 1958 with his article "Christianity and Contemporary Society."

His generation, Theotokas maintained, was much less willing to dismiss religious faith than were their elders, much more subdued and perplexed before the problems of good and evil, more aware of their inability to distinguish "what is ethically permissible and what is not—independent . . . of the restrictions of the penal code." The relationships of man to man and man to society had been weakened. Many reasons were offered for this corruption, but the most crucial, he believed, was the retreat of a religious consensus, which had left a spiritual vacuum "not only in the immorality and cynicism to be seen around us at every step, but in the anguish of men before the specter of death," an anguish that was responsible, he claimed, for "the wild compensations of ambition, of social ostentation, in the passion for material power, and in whatever intoxicates and helps us to forget the fact of death." Political and social ideologies, even though they may succeed in providing for the satisfaction of the individual's social and political needs, will still, he felt, leave him "alone and full of agony within chaos, confronting the death that awaits him."

The problem of belief is common to most people in our era, Theotokas believed, but the Greeks, besides the retreat of faith, must confront the problem of uniting their "divided heritage," the fusion of the two traditions of Christianity and Hellenism that, he stated, was done in a very glib manner by verbally yoking the two as "Helleno-Christian." These two words represent contrasting views of men. Classical humanism and Christian mysticism, moreover, had contributed twice to "spiritual crises," the first time in the fourteenth century in the controversy between Gregory Palamas and Barlaam, and the second time in a more profound and powerful crisis, in the fifteenth-century controversy between Gregory Gennadius and Gemistos Plethon. These differing traditions, Theotokas believed, were at permanent odds and can be ignored only when historical and political events, like the four-hundred year Turkish domination, suppressed them by concentrating within one institution, the church, for example, the hopes of a national liberation. With an established state, racial identity is no longer threatened and the essential contradictions of Hellenism and Christianity can no longer be overlooked.

The "central problem of contemporary man," however, which the Greek finds himself sharing is "the crisis of industrial civilization, which, on the one hand offers humanity unimaginable material conquests and promises men an unlimited prosperity and, on the other hand, threatens them with equally unlimited disasters."[3] The Greek, accustomed through the centuries of Turkish domination and during the decades of the early Greek state, to finding superficial solutions to his problems by "adopting the latest philosophic theory or literary and artistic school that dominated the large centers of Western Europe" now finds himself importing the same spiritual malaise that characterizes Western man. Just as Greece finds herself ground down between East and West politically, she is also confronted with a spiritual dilemma between the hateful totalitarianism of the Marxist East and the unsatisfying nihilism of the democratic West.

In "Exodus from Nihilism" he put forth the claim that the advances of science did not necessarily throw religious values into doubt. As in Latin countries Marxism and Christianity were not considered contradictory ideologies, so the acceptance of the Darwinian tenets and the findings of space research need not operate against the religious conception of life. Nihilism, however, is a direct attack upon "the Good News." Nietzsche's "death of God" and Sartre's brilliant but "deafening" repetition of the same insight set the tone for a nihilism that dominated the major European philosophic schools, international literary trends, American theater, new poetry, and contemporary painting and sculpture. But, in more ways than one, nihilism was a dead end which men would eventually reject. Theotokas found that the interest in Yoga, popular first in England and America, then in Europe, "threatened to alienate finally and irrevocably from his ethnic roots" whoever embraced these teachings. For those young Greeks who needed spiritual sustenance, Theotokas recommended an attempt at reinitiation into "their land's religious traditions, which have been for many centuries intertwined with the life of their people, with their national character, their temperament, their customs, [and] the memory of their fathers." This return to the cultural roots of a race was not unusual, Theotokas felt, for in literature, at least, it had been effected by "Eugene O'Neill, who accepted the Catholic Church of his Irish parents, T. S. Eliot, who returned to the Anglican Church of his distant forebears, and Boris Pasternak, who embraced the religious values of Holy Russia."

Foreigners who ignored the role of the Orthodox church in Greek life were apt to have a very superficial view of Greece,

Theotokas warned. In fact, returning to his familiar claim that
for many centuries Orthodoxy and Hellenism were synonymous,
he continued by asserting that an anticlerical political movement
could never exist in Greece, as it had elsewhere, and though "we
may often criticize the Church—at times with great severity—
we do so from within, as members . . . [and] not as though she
were a foreign body from which we want to separate ourselves."
Aside from this feeling of identity the Greek has with the Orthodox church there is the great tradition of Byzantine mysticism,
still alive on Mount Athos, which surpasses in significance and
profundity the corresponding expression of the West, but which
is ignored by the intellectuals of Greece, who have not exploited
or promoted it in their writings. The new historical conditions
will not demand that the Greek church take an active role in
patriotic struggles. The old identity of Orthodoxy and Hellenism
will slowly lose its coherence, and history will return the church
to its initial position as moral shepherd

in the spirit of the Fathers, but within a world totally new. . . . The
new historical conditions demand that the Church rediscover the
deeper sources of her spirituality and become again the home of a
pure and powerful spiritual life, to discuss ideas, to solve problems
of conscience, to offer noble examples of faith and virtue, to help
contemporary men give a meaning to their existence and [to] distinguish good from evil.[4]

II *The Constitutional Crisis*

This, conceivably, may have been the way George Theotokas
would have ended his days, aware of a spiritual dimension to a
life he had seen in his youth in strong sociopolitical terms, searching through a recently Westernized culture for a religious tradition that seemed to live only in monastic centers, and defending or explaining the status quo on those occasions when to do
so meant to earn the hostility of his fellow artists. As a patrician
by class, a democrat by temperament, and a thinker of the
Center-Left by position, Theotokas, in the early 1960s seemed
to be entering a calm harbor after a stormy lifetime of ideological turmoil. The "principle of human madness" that beguiled
him from his early fiction to *Invalids and Wayfarers* became less

playful and more significant, less a matter that made minor characters interesting caricatures and more a generalized aura that emanated from a source viewing human logic as a narrow, stultifying tool. In another country, Theotokas might have developed into a religious novelist, sharing an enlightened socio-political orientation with the progressive elements of this culture but basically dissatisfied with the shallowness of this view and dwelling more and more in a world of his imagination in which titanic issues of good and evil would be waged.

The events of July 15, 1965, pulled him back into the political realities he was slowly beginning to transcend. Once again Greece was in the midst of a political crisis, one that Theotokas clearly saw would lead to repression and dictatorship. King Constantine had dismissed the Prime Minister, George Papandreou, though the Center Union party had won a clear victory at the polls, and Theotokas, as he was about to confront what he was beginning to consider deeper issues, returned to the political arena with all the force of his honesty, his decency, and his eloquence in behalf of those democratic freedoms he had advocated all his life. It was to be this turmoil that was to dominate the remaining fifteen months of his life. Though on the threshold of a new way of looking at human aspiration and endeavor, Theotokas turned back to refight battles he thought had been won, and in an impressive series of articles that brought him a never-before experienced popularity, he articulated the values of the democratic man.

Theotokas was merely expressing ideas he had held all his life and he again found himself the vociferous opponent of the House of Glücksburg. Like the other, more illustrious royalty, they seemed to have forgotten nothing and learned nothing. When Herbert Kubly, an American writer who had gone to Greece to write an interpretive book about the country, was asked by Queen Frederika who his Greek friends were, he "pondered the question, wondering whom I should name," then mentioned George Theotokas.

"An intellectual," she said with scorn. "I don't like intellectuals. They're all weak and they have no courage. When my husband and I were fighting the Communists to save Greece, they sat in the cafes. They're still there and they're all against me."

If the enemy to Greek freedom in the 1960s was obscurantism and a royal coup d'etat, the defender of democracy was a politician with "a politician's faults" who had made "a politician's mistakes." But the party led by George Papandreou was, according to Theotokas, "the only hope, the only party that represents the people of Greece, that cares for the future. The majority has a right to rule. You cannot say, because you disagree with it, that a majority cannot be trusted to rule, that it is incapable."

Convinced that the Center Union's concept of democracy in Greece was similar to that of the United States, at least the United States he had known since the Depression and the New Deal, Theotokas was genuinely upset at the machinations of the United States Embassy, which he could view from his study window across Boulevard Vasilisis Sophias, in working with the governments that succeeded one another with dismal regularity after Papandreou was dismissed. The rightist groups clustered around the King, he stated,

will not voluntarily give up their power. Since they know Papandreou's popularity, they delay an election as long as possible. As a last resort they would establish military rule. This is a very real danger. Toward this end there are frequent dismissals of nonloyal officers, a tightening of the ruling circle. The King is in command of the army, which he believes he controls, but an army is made up of young men from the villages and the islands, and no one can tell what they might do.[5]

The problem, as Theotokas viewed it, was that the conservative forces in Greek society had not kept pace with the times but had remained in the "cultural and social attitudes of central and eastern Europe in the era of Kaiser Wilhelm II" fighting with "blind passion . . . every attempt to renew themselves, even the most politically moderate reformation, *insisting that the country be kept back to where they (still) are.*"

The principle of corruption of which he had become aware in theological terms and which, because of the seeming stability of Greek life in the early 1960s, was apparent only in social and interpersonal relationships, suddenly appeared in the political sphere as a retrogressive force that wanted to restore Greece to the pre–World War I era by every means, "legitimate or illegitimate." This force was the Greek Right, "that many-tentacled complex of various forces, obvious or hidden," which denied the political solution that Theotokas himself had always advocated, namely, that "the democratic system in Greece [be allowed to] function properly, [that] the people [be allowed to] vote freely and that their decision be respected."

He accused the leaders of current Greece, "men of the Court, politicians, economists, and others who essentially direct [the Greek] national fate" of being interested only in the maintenance of ephemeral power, unable to view ahead to see what the consequences were of their decision to "destroy the unity of the Center." It was this democratic center, with all its weaknesses, that, according to Theotokas, was the strongest guarantee the Right had for security and stability. This dismissal of the majority opinion in such a thoughtless and even lighthearted way Theotokas termed a new phenomenon, "a political nihilism" that "corresponds to the contemporary schools of philosophy, literature, and the theater, which are possessed by the sense of nothingness, of hollowness, and of the absurd in life."

Leading without leadership, the decision-making cliques that wield power without public mandate seem not to care that they were leaving the nation to the "whims of fortune, as in 1920–1922" in a Mediterranean and a Middle East characterized by instability and simmering war and in a larger world dominated by nations which concerned themselves solely with their own national interests.

Finding Greek society divided by great differences in wealth and poverty, Theotokas called for reforms that would develop the economy and increase national productivity so that all Greeks could be assured of useful employment and the satisfaction of their basic needs. This, he felt, presupposed a state that was essentially democratic and "up-to-date, bold and creative" governments that would dislodge Greece from her "sterile conservatism." He demanded, in other words, a "New Deal" for Greece, distressed that the Center Union was unable to fulfill, in the space of a year or so, more than the needed educational reforms, unable to offer anything more than a hope for something better. But it was this hope, this promise for continued and gradual improvement "that wakened in the conservative portion of our society the panic fear that darkened [its] conscience."[6]

Theotokas knew what was happening, though the men with whom he had temporarily identified himself in the early 1960s seemed to misread the clues. Were they corrupt, or merely unwise, despite their intellectual accomplishments and erudition? A little of both, perhaps, and Theotokas, as he saw the political situation rapidly deteriorating, did not disguise his suspicions of their motives. Of the same patrician class as he, they were men with whom he had just discovered that he had nothing in common but class and education. They feared communism so much, he complained, that they saw it everywhere, ignoring the fact that Greece was locked into the intricate system of Western alliance and that even during the December battles in 1944 the Russian force under Tolboukin, at the Greek border, did not cross into Greece because of the agreement between Churchill and Stalin at Yalta. When leaders of the Right like DeGaulle envisioned a united Europe, why did men like Panayotis Kanellopoulos, he asked, insist on dwelling in an atmosphere of fear and suspicion? It had been out of a similar climate that General Metaxas staged his coup. "We should not sleep too peacefully," Theotokas concluded.[7]

It was intellectuals of the Right like Kanellopoulos, Petros Haris, and Constantine Tsatsos, the president of the Academy of Athens, whom Theotokas accused of being, unwittingly perhaps, apologists of a dictatorship he saw darkening the horizon. Tsatsos had attacked Marios Ploritis with extremely personal abuse in a morning paper of the Right and accused him and Theotokas of defending a government merely because it was politic to do so. Theotokas responded by admitting that his group, who were so few they could "fit in one taxi cab," would probably suffer for their stand, whereas Tsatsos, who he said had always done what was politic and accordingly made a 180 degree turn "from the socialism of his youth to liberalism to reaction [had] been rewarded for it accordingly."[8]

It was these intellectual spokesmen of the Right and the leaders, visible and invisible, of the "events of July and its consequences" whom Theotokas warned. One morning, he predicted, all Greeks would wake up to discover that "new men [were] ruling them, unknown men with strange ideas." The dictatorship they would impose, though it would not "be justified by

history, by economic necessities, or by any of the usual reasons,"
would "do away with all human rights, all traditional processes
and safeguards." This violent overthrow, Theotokas stated, would
be as much of a surprise to the Right as to the other Greeks.
Even though men of the Right might try to create an atmosphere
of tension and fear, because it helped them to maintain control,
they did not really believe that a civil war or a revolution was
possible any longer, for none of the conditions that applied in
December of 1944 applied now: there was stability at the border,
Greece was part of the Atlantic Alliance, there were no armed
partisans within Greece, and there existed a "strong and zealous
police force." What Greece needed, he maintained, was not fear
or hysteria but "a free environment" that would permit the
problems to be identified so that they might be solved.[9]

The Right, in refusing to accept this characterization and
identifying itself with nationalism and all its enemies—no matter
what their actual position was in the political spectrum—as
"Communists," was merely trying to deny the existence of a
Center, a moderate political position interested in actual reforms.
By dismissing the Center as a "Trojan horse" for the ambitions
of the extreme Left, and by demanding that those of this per-
suasion decide clearly between themselves and the "Popular
Front," the men of the Right sought "to maintain . . . in Greece"
Theotokas unequivocably stated, "an atmosphere of Civil War, so
that we will continue indefinitely to live with the spirit of
December, 1944."

But what is the Greek Right? Though he never disguised his
thoughts out of fear or caution, Theotokas found himself writing
in the daily newspaper, that most open of all forums for a mass
audience, and he must, out of the logic of history, be the one
to formulate clearly an answer to this troublesome question.
This Right that refused to accept its appellation but preferred
to be called Nationalist was, after the King's coup, composed of

. . . followers of monarchy, men of the dictatorship of the Fourth of
August, collaborators of the German occupier, reactionary politicians
of the anti-Venizelist school, fanatical educational obscurantists, mad
neofascists and, among them, various ex-liberals and democrats who
never cease to show their change of heart toward their past.[10]

During this period of rage, Theotokas subjected the church to a criticism that would have surprised even himself a few months earlier. A defender of the Orthodox church in the recent past, Theotokas always felt that the church's reactionary position on many issues was a major obstacle to its attainment of relevance. He treasured, however, its venerable traditions, the liturgy, the monastic communities, and the ethical and psychological verities it promulgated. These, he felt, could be divorced from its social role, which he demanded be enlightened and modernized. The close identification of the Orthodox church with the Greek state he again began to see as oligarchic, but he believed that reaction was not a corollary to its essentially conservative nature. Far from advocating the attitude of the Greek church men, Theotokas viewed the role of the hierarchy in bleak and unsparing terms. In Europe, the Roman Catholic church was being renewed with the Vatican Councils, and the ecumenical movement was forging a new attitude within a fragmented Christianity, but nothing of this seemed to be reflected in the Greek church, which was so far behind the times that the least it could do, he observed in melancholy, was to try to be Christian.[11]

III The Bells

The product of his final year of life, *The Bells*, is the fruition in fiction of the years during which he considered the issues of God and death and the problem of evil. These concerns had developed gradually, making their first appearance in the dramatic works he wrote during the Occupation and reaching intensity with the death of loved ones, after which he publicly pursued and investigated the religious view of life. Politics had always been his passion, and his position had not essentially changed from the time of his youth, but his deepening religious interests compelled him to reassess his interpretation of the motives, the ambitions, and the flaws of men. *The Bells* shows Theotokas grappling with the issue of original sin and its role in the downfall of civilizations.

Kostis Philomatis, the central character, is a strong-willed rationalist who has worked his way out of the poverty of his youth to the directorship of a leading bank in Athens and an international reputation as an economist. Something, however, happens to him on a brief trip to New York, where he has gone to negotiate an important loan that will fund a major plan he has for the Greek economy. He returns to Athens a changed man, behaving toward his wife in a contradictory manner, by turns violent and unusually passive, and weeping at films when he had not even cried at his parents' funerals. He has withered somehow, as though he has lost confidence in himself and the values that previously motivated his life. All this the reader learns when Smaragda, Philomatis's wife, goes to Karolos Dandalos, a famed Athenian psychiatrist, and tells him of Kostis's behavior. Dandalos, after seeing the economist, will not name "that" from which Philomatis suffers, since the terminology changes, he says, and laymen find it difficult to understand, but, like Joan d'Arc and Moses, he hears "things." Kostis Philomatis hears bells.

Despite Dandalos's assurance that some psychiatric help is possible, the reader sees, when he is provided with a first-person view of Philomatis, that what seems obviously the result of overwork, sleeplessness, and ambition is much deeper and more complex. It is a crisis of middle age, certainly, and Smaragda, in spite of her beauty, cannot help but be jealous of the attraction Nora, her husband's secretary, has for him. It is, moreover, the hollowness of achievement, the perpetual threat to the Faustian man who attains what he has always sought. Mental breakdown would describe it all too neatly, perhaps, for Kostis Philomatis is preoccupied with other issues. His troubled mind confounds the bells he hears at the strangest moments with the hallucination that famed cities are being destroyed before his eyes; these two events he attributes to the presence of a mysterious, slightly absurd, fat man named Doctor Snak. He is evil, of course, and it is to discover the source of evil that Philomatis abandons wife, home, and position to track down his theological quarry.

Doctor Snak is the reason things fall apart. He is the principle of corruption and evil that Kostis Philomatis was too busy and too insulated by his rationalism to accept before. Snak is everything and everywhere. Dressed in black, with silvery hair, rosy cheeks, and skin like well-scrubbed porcelain, he appears to

Philomatis like an hallucination at every scene of chaos: when the buildings of Rockefeller Center sway and collapse in rubble, when the Seine floods and destroys Paris, when the North Pole crushes Stockholm, when a colossal wind strikes the Acropolis in Athens and sweeps the Rock clean. This is the world of Philomatis, the West that nurtured him, a civilization now going the way of Karnak, Knossos, Thebes, Troy, Babylon, Rome, and Byzantium. It is Snak who runs off from every scene of destruction, "like a rabbit, fat and jocular, holding his briefcase firmly in one hand and clutching his hat tightly to his head with the other." He is the "dreg of the dregs," the one responsible for all evil, and Philomatis tries to track him down.

The disappearance of Philomatis, who goes off initially with his secretary, becomes a cause for scandal in the Athenian press, at first of a superficial nature and then of a more serious sort. This is particularly true when Nora returns alone, silent as to her employer's exact whereabouts in the Middle East. Foreign interests are involved apparently, and the Athenian press commentators have a field day wondering about the role of oil interests, the CIA, the British, the Russians, the Israelis, the Arabs. Somehow, Doctor Snak's name is unearthed and speculation links his appearance with colossal trusts, Great Powers, missile bases, fleet movements. The fact that Philomatis was in a fight in a Cairo cafe with someone he called Snak becomes known. Then the economist is found dead on Mount Sinai.

After the funeral of his patient, Dandalos goes on a hunt for clues and concludes his search at Mount Sinai in the cave of the Monk Pachomios, who had often seen the seriously troubled Philomatis. According to him, the economist was obsessed by certain incidents in the Old Testament, had arguments with a certain Doctor Snak, and was tormented by nightmarish fantasies about the destruction of great cities. The last time he was seen, Philomatis had been going up to the Peak of Horeb. He seemed, according to the Bedouin who witnessed it all, to be fighting with someone who was not visible. Philomatis evidently lost his balance and fell to his death.

The evidence within the novel compels the reader to believe that Philomatis is undergoing a mental crisis that leads him to madness and death. Yet, the character of his preoccupations and

their profundity place him firmly within the religious tradition
of Christianity, for he is searching for the source of evil in man,
an evil superior to man's mind, threatening the orderliness of
his instincts.

As we learn from "Dialogue at Han Halili," a document Pachomios gives Dandalos from the economist's effects, the evil, the
disorientation that manifests itself as a mental breakdown in
Philomatis, has more than theological cause. There is a political
cause as well, one that stems from man as a social being, from the
institutions he has created to order his life. It is the nothingness,
the *nihil,* that has grown as much as the universe has expanded,
Snak tells Philomatis:

"... The evil road that men took, they took all together. To discuss
who is more to blame and who less, who can claim extenuating cir-
cumstances and who cannot, is to quibble. The fact is that if men
wanted to they could have stopped at some point. They would have
raised their hands and said, 'We'll go no further. This road leads to
chaos.' Who would have been able to force them to continue ad-
vancing? But they wished to go, the road appealed to them. What
irresistible force, I wonder, compelled and continues to compel them?
The glow of wealth? The passion for leadership, the pleasure of
power? Vanity? Monumental egotism? The deep, dark, mass instincts?
But what is the use of analyzing these things further? I told you, it's
too late. Let's share the guilt. Soon, it will be closing time."[12]

The bells signify the danger Philomatis sees before the political and social life of Greece and of the West, alarming sounds
that break into his iron-clad rationalism and make him fear the
worst from an enemy no one else can see. Doctor Snak is the
eternal principle of evil, the Devil, the Snake, circulating in the
world and among people who assign different causes to the
acts for which he is responsible.

That Theotokas would write such a novel at the end of his
life is perhaps the most significant comment he could have made
about his despair at the political situation of Greece. Thoughtful
men and women knew that the constitutional crisis Greece was
in as a result of the King's dismissal of the Prime Minister would
have appalling repercussions, but there seemed to be no way
of bringing together the polarized political communities.

Theotokas died six months before the coup he had clearly foretold took place, the sounds of whose "bells" woke Philomatis out of the deep slumber of optimistic rationalism, out of trust in the "Project" whose funding on Wall Street would bring progress and happiness to Greece. The funeral of Theotokas, held on Monday, October 31, 1966, at the First Cemetery of Athens, attended as it was by men and women of the political, literary, and artistic worlds, was the occasion for an impassioned assessment of his contributions to modern Greek culture. Since it brought together men and women of the democratic Right and of the Left as well as of the Center, it emphasized the nonpartisan nature of the search for truth by dialogue, for which he had always stood.[13]

Notes and References

Preface

1. He had also written verse, gathered in several collections, but made no claims for himself as a poet.

Chapter One

1. G. Perastikos, "Theotokas," *Neoellinika Grammata*, Nov. 20, 1937, pp. 12–14. *Idem. Elefthero Pnevma* (Free Spirit) (Athens: Rhallis, 1929), pp. 102–3.

2. See Constantine Dimaras's *Istoria Tis Neoellinikis Logotechnias* (History of Modern Greek Literature), 3rd edition (Athens: Ikaros, 1964), p. 376. An English translation of the 4th edition by Mary P. Gianos was published by the State University of New York Press in 1972.

3. He exempts Constantine Theotokis's *Tourkoyiannos* in *O Katadikos* (The Convict) from this stricture.

4. P. 121.

5. C. Dimaras, ed. *Elefthero Pnevma* (Free Spirit) (Athens: Hermes, 1973), p. xxxii.

6. *Ekpaideftikos Omilos*, a lobby founded by demoticists in 1910, which, at its inception, was composed of thinkers whose politics represented all shades of the spectrum.

7. Theotokas, "Psycharis," in *Pnevmatiki Poreia* (Intellectual Journey) (Athens: Fexis, 1961), p. 201.

8. It is instructive to witness the first appearance in *Idea, Proia, Nea Grammata*, and *Neoellinika Grammata* of writers who became members of the generation. Theotokas himself reviewed the books of Thanasis Petsalis, George Seferis, M. Karagatsis, Tatiana Stavrou, Kosmas Politis, Stelios Xefloudas, Ilias Venezis, and Stratis Myrivilis.

9. *Idea* vol. I, no. 1, Jan., 1933.

10. "A Lovable Thinker," *Kyklos*, I, no. 2 (Dec. 1931), 89–90.

11. *Idea* I, no. 5 (May, 1933), 408.

12. Theotokas, "Our Language," *Intellectual Journey*, p. 313.

13. *Kyklos* I, no. 1 (Nov., 1931), 30.

14. *Idea* I, no. 5 (May, 1933), 285–89.

15. *Idea* I, no. 2 (Feb., 1933), 101–7. An interesting portrait of Varnalis can be found in Bert Britles's forgotten *Exiles in the Aegean*, a fine study of the political events in Greece between 1935–1938. For students who are curious about the Metaxas jails, this is an invaluable source by an adventurous Australian journalist who clearly identifies himself with the Left.

16. *Idea* I, no. 4 (April, 1933), 253–57.

17. *Idea* I, no. 7 (July, 1933), 61–62.

18. *Idea* I, no. 6 (June, 1933), 408.

19. *Embros sto Koinoniko Provlima* (Forward to the Social Problem) (Athens: Pyrsos, 1932), pp. 12–13.

20. It is significant that he does not include this essay in *Intellectual Journey*, 1961.

21. *Forward.*, p. 26.

22. Supranationalism always fascinated Theotokas, and we will see how it became a major theme in his discursive writing, an idea he pursued through his travels to Europe, the Soviet Union, and the United States.

23. *Forward.*, pp. 52–53.

Chapter Two

1. *Ores Argias* (Leisure Hours) (Athens: Estia, 1931).

2. (*The Logbook of Argo and the Daemon*) (Athens: Pyrsos, 1939).

3. It has been published in English by Methuen (1951) in a translation by Ares Tsatsopoulos and E. Margaret Brooke.

4. *Argo* (Athens: Estia, 1956), 3rd edition, p. 32.

5. Originally, at the stage of conception, *Argo* was to be entitled *The Daemon*. Theotokas discussed his ideas about the novel with Stelios Xefloudas in Paris in 1928. He set it aside, though, and went to London in 1929 where he wrote *Free Spirit* and continued his studies. *Leisure Hours*, also written in London, intervened, as did the writing of three plays, *Eve*, *Force*, and *The Turks*, all aborted efforts. The novel began to develop as he considered it, and one day, at the Zappeion, a man who must have been Nikos Kazantzakis (he is identified in *Logbook* by the initials N.K., and there is abundant evidence to prove that Theotokas and Kazantzakis knew each other well at that time) told him that the "revolutionary student," who was to have hailed from the Peloponessos, "should come from the City," i.e., Constantinople. "It will be a good opportunity for you to exploit your childhood memories from the world of the City and thus enrich your book." See entry (6), December 14, 1933, in *Logbook*.

6. *Argo,* pp. 50–51.
7. *Neoellinika Grammata* I, no. 23 (Sept. 15, 1935), 3.

Chapter Three

1. Theotokas, "George Seferis as I knew him," *Epoches,* no. 10 (Feb., 1964), pp. 11–17.
2. The first essay on Seferis that Karandonis published was in 1931, when he was twenty-one years old and when Seferis had published only *Strophe* (Turning Point) and a few scattered poems. In 1936 Karandonis published *George Seferis, The Poet.*
3. *Ta Nea Grammata* I, no. 1 (Jan., 1935), 48. The note, on a page entitled "Chronicles," which it shares with the notice of the death of Fotos Politis the previous December, was written but not initialed by Karandonis.
4. The Academy was congratulated, however, in the same issue, no. 5 (May, 1935), p. 328, for deciding to publish a complete edition of the works of Solomos. *Nea Grammata* recommends G. Spatalas and N. Tomadakis as directors of the undertaking. References to Ouranis can be found in no. 2, pp. 119–20; no. 5, pp. 324–27; and no. 6, p. 392; to Malakasis and Panayotopoulos in no. 5, pp. 324–27; and to Haris, vol. III, no 2, pp. 165–67. Ouranis wrote in *Nea Estia,* no. 194. The conflict between Haris and Karandonis was over the decision of the former to erect a bust of Kostis Palamas, but it was merely a continuation of their old squabble. Theotokas resigned from the committee formed under the initiative of *Nea Estia* (he had accepted over the telephone), because he realized that the bust had become the object of a discreditable squabble. His letter of resignation was published in *Neoellinika Grammata,* Feb. 6, 1937, p. 2.
5. "Chronicles-Recapitulation," uninitialed but by Karandonis, *Nea Grammata* II, no. 1, (Jan. 1936), 85–86. *Nea Grammata* lasted until spring 1940. There were only three issues in 1939: Nos. 1–3 (Jan.–March), Nos. 4–6 (April–June), and Nos. 7–12 (July–Dec.). The last issue was spring 1940. With the Greco-Italian War, of course, publication ceased. The periodical began again in 1944 and lasted six issues, beginning from January to July; a double issue was published on July of 1945 before folding. Its place was taken over by *Anglo-Elliniki Epitheorisi* (Anglo-Greek Review), which began publishing in 1945.
6. The slogan of the "Popular" Party of Greece, and the title of an ideological journal (directed by Aristos Kambanis) dedicated to promoting its ideals. The periodical *To Neon Kratos* was founded in 1937.

7. *Nea Grammata* I, nos. 7–8 (July–August, 1935), 444.

8. Alexander Delmouzos, among other things, provided with his experimental school in Volos a model for the educational reform that became the basis of the pedagogical reformation under Venizelos, 1917–1920. Panagis Lorenzatos, professor of Ancient Greek at the University of Athens from 1924 to 1935, wrote *The Homeric Lexicon*. Nicholas Bëes was professor of Byzantine and Modern Greek Literature, and an academician. Haralambos Theodoridis, wrote *Introduction to Philosophy* and *Epicurus: The True Aspect of the Ancient World*. Yiannis Apostolakis was a scholar of the demotic song and wrote *Poetry in our Life, Aristotles Valaoritis, Krystallis and the Folk Song*, and *The Klephtic Song*.

9. "Freedom and Force," *Idea* I, no. 5 (May, 1933), 285, including footnote.

10. The last two issues of *Nea Grammata* before the hiatus had both been double numbers. June's—nos. 5 and 6—was the Special Commemorative on Palamas and July's was nos. 7 and 8. Theotokas finished the year 1936, vol. II, with essays on Palamas and Tigrane Yergate, and is represented only by "Everything's in Order," his best short story, in 1937.

11. Notably in the essays of George Seferis. See the author's essay "The Strategy of George Seferis: The Individual Poet and the Greek Tradition," *The Texas Quarterly* XI, no. 4 (Winter 1968), 72–88.

12. "Dickens," *Neoellinika Grammata*, April 24, 1937, p. 4.

13. "Exchanges," *Neoellinika Grammata*, July 31, 1937, p. 5.

14. *Ibid.*

15. This important critique can be found, only slightly altered in form, in Andreas Karandonis's *Prose Writers and Prose Works of the Generation of the Thirties*, a collection of essay-reviews on the work of selected writers. It is by no means exhaustive or synthetic. The essay on Theotokas's *Argo*, concluded on p. 109, is dated 1938. This is a mistake. Karandonis published the study of Theotokas's work up to *Argo* in *Nea Grammata*, vol. III, nos. 10 and 11; the latter was published in November, 1937.

16. The first quotation comes from p. 108, while the second and third come from page 66 of "Theotokas" in *Prose Writers*.

17. For example, in the same essay, he says "For a novelist, who is interested in the total vision of life, politics can never be a theme as fecund and as exciting as love," pp. 100–101.

18. Karandonis, *op. cit.*, p. 80.

19. *Ibid.*, p. 94. This runs counter to the fact that Theotokas was in trouble with the Ministry of Education and was scolded by Professor Andreadis on the day of his examination. See chapter 1.

20. *Ibid.*, p. 97.

21. *Ibid.*, p. 103.

22. *Ibid.*, pp. 89–92.

23. "A Strange Criticism," *Nea Grammata* IV, nos. 1–3 (Jan.–Mar., 1938) 13–14. The Galaxias edition to which I've also referred follows basically the text of *Nea Grammata* but with fewer works, without the commentary of Yiannopoulos's contemporaries, and without the thorough bibliography of George Katsimbalis. It has, however, the significant inclusion of those passages edited from the journal by the Metaxas censors, notably the anti-German comments in "Greek color." All references to the Yiannopoulos controversy will be to the edition of his works in *Nea Grammata*.

24. "Toward the Greek Renaissance," *Nea Grammata* IV (Jan.–Mar., 1938), 23–27.

25. "Xenomania," *Nea Grammata* IV (Jan.–Mar., 1938), 40. The discussion on Greek music can be found in "Greek Music, Forward," pp. 28–40.

26. "Contemporary Painting," *Nea Grammata* IV (Jan.–Mar., 1938), 90–91.

27. Aristos Kambanis, "Reminiscence," *Nea Grammata* IV (Jan.–Mar., 1938), 241–54 and 262.

28. On horseback, his body anointed with perfumes, he galloped into the sea at Skaramanga wearing a garland of wild flowers and firing a revolver into his forehead. Gregory Xenopoulos claims that Yiannopoulos was reduced to giving away his books because he could not sell them; this at a time when he was penniless.

29. "Chronicles," *Nea Grammata* IV (Jan.–Mar., 1938), 294–95.

30. *Neoellinika Grammata*, May 21, 1938, p. 5.

31. Prokopiou identifies Yiannopoulos's influences as Hippolyte Taine's *The Philosophy of Art in Greece*, which is physiocratic in that it bases its study of Greek aesthetics on the Greek landscape, and French Impressionism, which demanded that the artist leave his studio and go out into nature to paint. I don't think anyone had pointed out the influence of D'Annunzio except Kambanis.

32. *Neoellinika Grammata*, "The Example of Yiannopoulos," pp. 4–14.

33. *Nea Grammata* IV, nos. 4–5 (Apr.–May, 1938), 430–31.

34. Odysseus Elytis, in *Nea Grammata*, IV, nos. 6–7 (June–July, 1938), 581–84 refers to an article entitled "The Dangers of Half-Learning" in the previous issue and states that he likes Theotokas and his *Argo*, not because it sold out two printings but because there are some moving pages in it. The Theotokas-Elytis controversy enters the highly interesting terrain of surrealism, which the poet defends

and which Theotokas tries to interpret in economic, historical, and social terms.

35. "Letter from Theotokas," *Neoellinika Grommata*, June 11, 1938, p. 9.

36. *Ibid.*, pp. 1–2. I translated *xefteria* as "whizzes."

37. *Neoellinika Grammata*, June 18, 1938, pp. 1–3. Lead article.

38. *Ibid.*, p. 6.

39. K. M. Michalidis considers Yiannopoulos "the greatest thinker and writer of his time."

40. "The Issue of Greekness of Spirit and Art," *Neoellinika Grammata*, Dec. 17, 1938, pp. 1–2.

Chapter Four

1. *Euripides Pendozalis and Other Stories* (Athens: Pyrsos, 1937). A second edition was published by Themelio in October, 1966.

2. There are others besides these, notably Frixos Avgoustis in *Invalids and Wayfarers*.

3. "Everything's in Order" in *Euripides Pendozalis and Other Stories*. This story was first published in *Nea Grammata*, III, no. 4 (April, 1937), 274–91.

4. "Therapeia" was first published in *Idea*, July, 1933, pp. 22–29; "The Gang" in *Neoellinika Grammata*, Jan. 16, 1937, pp. 3–4; and "The Garden with the Cypresses" also in *Neoellinika Grammata*, Mar. 13, 1937, pp. 3–11.

5. *To Daimonio* (The Daemon) (Athens: 1938). I consulted the 1961 edition by Fexis publishers and all references will be to that edition.

6. *Leonis*, 2nd edition (Athens: Ikaros, 1946). An interview of Theotokas by Th. Ziogas appeared in *Neoellinika Grammata*, Sept. 2, 1939, p. 12, where he states that he worked on a "novel about adolescence in Constantinople" for five weeks the previous summer while on a trip to Chios. He finished ten chapters and thought he had ten more to write. *Leonis* has twenty-two. Chapter 3 of *Leonis* was printed in the Feb. 17, 1940 issue of *Neoellinika Grammata*, pp. 1–5. A note accompanying the excerpt states that "barring an event beyond his will" (i.e., the war), the author will publish a novel that should be ready by the end of the year. Chapter 17 was printed in the Sept. 7, 1940 issue of *Neoellinika Grammata*, pp. 1–5, with a note that the book is to circulate shortly.

Chapter Five

1. The interested reader is directed to the author's essay "The Contemporary Greek Theater" (To Synchrono Neoelliniko Theatro)

(Athens: Kedros, 1970) that introduced to the Greek reading public the work of six young dramatists in a paperback series. More available to American readers, perhaps, is the author's essay "Loula Anagnostaki and the New Theater of Greece," *Chicago Review* 21, no. 2 (August, 1969), pp. 83–87.

2. All references in this chapter to plays written by Theotokas will be to the two volumes of *Theatrika Erga*, of which vol. I contains what he calls *Neoelliniko Laïko Theatro* and vol. II contains *Erga Diafora*.

3. Written in 1942 and published in *Theatro*, 1944. It was admired by Kazantzakis who wrote to Theotokas of its impact on him and his decision to write a play of his own on Capodistrias. The significance of this became apparent when Theotokas became Director of the National Theater and decided to stage the Kazantzakis play. See *Neoelliniko Laïko Theatro*, vol. I, p. 400.

4. Written in 1943–44 and published as *Byzantine Night* in *Nea Estia*, vol. 39, in 1946, although it is most recently entitled *I Lakaina*.

5. For this whole story, see Theotokas's article, "The First Post-War Period of the National Theater," *Nea Estia*, 39, no. 451 (April 15, 1946), 460–73 and Alex. Argyriou's study, "George Theotokas: His Intellectual Presence in Modern Greek Letters," *Epitheorisi Technis*, no. 146 (Feb., 1967), pp. 126–27.

6. Alkis Thrylos, "George Theotokas: The Climate of Intellectual Play and Virtue," *Nea Estia* 53, no. 617 (March 15, 1953), 368.

7. Theotokas, "Theater in Contemporary Greece," *Nea Estia* 65, no. 758 (Feb. 1, 1959), pp. 168–77.

8. *Vima*, Sept. 3, 1961. The historical material concerning the founding of the National Theater of Northern Greece can be found in the "Prologue" to Socrates Karandinos's *Saranta Chronia Theatro* (Forty Years of Theater) vol. III (Athens, 1971).

Chapter Six

1. *Sto Katofli ton Neon Kairon* (On the Threshold of the New Era) (Athens: Ikaros, 1944). My references are to the edition in *Intellectual Journey*, p. 10.

2. "The Sun of Freedom," *Nea Estia* 36, nos. 415–416 (Sept. 15– Nov. 1, 1944), 798–99.

3. "On the Subject of Communism," *Nea Estia* 44, no. 512 (Nov. 1, 1948), pp. 1334–39.

4. *Dokimio Gia tin Ameriki* (Essay on America) (Athens: Ikaros, 1954).

5. *Provlimata tou Kairou mas* (Problems of Our Time) (Athens: Ikaros, 1956).

6. *Taxidia stin Mesi Anatoli kai ston Agion Oro* (Travels to the Middle East and to Mount Athos) (Athens: Fexis, 1961). Quotation is in chapter 7, "What the Monastery of Sinai Contains."

Chapter Seven

1. *The Sacred Road*, vol. I of *Invalids and Wayfarers* (Athens: Estia, 1964), pp. 163–64.

2. *The Sacred Road*: "A Wind of madness blew through the world but it wasn't a bad thing" (p. 26). And: "All ideologies are based on the axiom that man is basically a rational being. . . . What we need is an ideology based on the presupposition of humanity's madness. The Theory of Silent Human Madness" (pp. 92–93). The theme of madness explicitly stated in this manner does not appear in the second volume: it is a theme that all the characters illustrate in their actions and thoughts.

3. *The Sacred Road*, Prologue, p. 7.

4. The second volume of *Invalids and Wayfarers* contains the following: Part Two, "The Archives of the Monk Timotheos," which is composed of 'The Notebooks of Monk Timotheos,' 'The Letters of Theano to Marinos,' 'The Deposition of Aegisilaos Pandelidis,' and 'Letters of Kyriakos to Marinos.' Part Three, a much shorter section, is entitled 'The Survivors' and resembles the attempts of nineteenth-century novelists to inform their readership about the lives of the characters after the major fictional event.

5. Theotokas, although he tried countless times to avoid a direct admission of this, was clearly influenced strongly by the EAM execution of the tragedienne Eleni Papadaki, during the December battles.

Chapter Eight

1. By 1963 the social, political, and economic conditions were such that a serious journal of some quality could be relatively certain of success. Under the general editorship of Angelos Terzakis, *Epoches* began a splendid career that lasted until the coup of April 21, 1967 and its censorship put an end to intellectual questioning. Theotokas, along with men like Dimaras, Skalioras, Karapanagiotis, and Christos Lambrakis (the publisher), was on the editorial board that guided *Epoches* to a preeminent position in Greek publishing, bringing the Greek reader month by month the most enlightened and penetrating writing by native and foreign authors. *Epoches* was to be the forum for the intellectuals and artists of the democratic center, an organ for the confrontation with the most advanced ideas of Greece and of the rest of the world.

2. Letter by Kay Cicellis in *Epoches*, no. 4, August, 1963. The writers just emerging into general recognition were Costas Taktsis, Vasilis Vasilikos, Nikos Kasdaglis, Nikos Kachtitsis, Alexander Kotzias, Rodis Roufos, Galateia Sarandi, Nikos Gabriel Pentzikis, and Yiannis Beratis. The Savidis and Daphnis letters are in *Epoches*, no. 3, July 1963, pp. 80–82, while Theotokas's last letter is in the August, 1963 issue.

3. Theotokas, "Christianity and the Greeks," from "Return to the Roots" collected in *Intellectual Journey (Pnevmatiki Poreia)* p. 143.

4. Theotokas, "The Destiny of Orthodoxy," *ibid.*, p. 154.

5. Herbert Kubly, *Gods and Heroes* (London: Gollancz, 1970). This quotation is from p. 233, while the previous two are from pp. 100–101.

6. Theotokas, *The National Crisis* (Athens: Themelio, 1966). The characterization of the Right as Central European can be found in the prologue, p. 10. The next two quotes are from "The Hope," pp. 17–18. The correspondence of nihilism to the effort to destroy the Center is from "Whither Are We Headed?" p. 21, while Theotokas's suspicions of his fellows can be found in "The Deeper Reasons for the Crisis," p. 40.

7. "Expectations and Dangers," *Vima*, Thursday, Jan. 27, 1966, p. 1.

8. Editor of *Nea Estia*, Petros Haris, writing in an article entitled "Two Worlds" in *Eleftheria*, Sept. 30, 1965 attacked Theotokas for involving himself in the "political arena" after the events of July. Theotokas, criticized for mixing art with politics, interpreted this as a public insult and stated that he did not want "to belong to the same literary circle as Mr. Haris." Both men were members of the "Group of Twelve," a literary group devoted to awarding prizes for the best achievements in various genres for the year. Theotokas consequently resigned from the "Group of Twelve" in a letter dated Oct. 3, 1965, and published in *Vima* of Oct. 6, 1965, p. 2. As of Thursday, April 7, 1966, the "Twelve" included Tasos Athanasiadis, Ilias Venezis, Constantine Dimaras, Andreas Karandonis, Stelios Xefloudas, Alkis Thrylos, I. M. Panayotopoulos, D. Stassinopoulos, Petros Haris, and Yiannis Hadzinis. Ploritis's letter is in *Vima* of Oct. 2, 1966, p. 8 and Theotokas's defense of him in Saturday's paper, Oct. 8, 1966, p. 1.

9. Theotokas, "The Dictatorship," *Vima*, Sunday, Feb. 20, 1966, pp. 1–6.

10. Theotokas, "National Perspective," *The National Crisis*, pp. 54–56.

11. Theotokas, "The Church in our Time: The Intellectual Horizon in Greece is Limited," *Vima*, Sunday, April 10, 1966, pp. 1–6.

12. *I Kambanes* (The Bells) (Athens: Estias, 1970), p. 128. The novel ran serially in *Vima* from Dec. 4, 1966 to Jan. 1, 1967.

13. After the funeral of Theotokas, Petros Haris, the publisher of *Nea Estia*, reprinted the eulogies of Ilias Venezis and Evangelos Papanoutsos, the latter citing him for his constant fight for democratic liberties. (*Nea Estia* 80, no. 945 [Nov. 15, 1966], 1671–72.) In the spirit of the occasion, Haris promises "many more pages devoted to George Theotokas." The aftermath of the *coup d'etat* of April 21, 1967, found *Nea Estia* still publishing, though every other periodical —literary or otherwise—had shut down in protest to the censorship, yet the pages devoted to Theotokas had, after seven years, not appeared, although there have been issues dedicated to Spyros Melas, Charles Baulelaire, and Dimitris Kokkinos. The work of some men, it seems, is such that not even a fragment can be taken from it and rendered harmless.

Selected Bibliography

PRIMARY SOURCES

1. Imaginative Prose

Ores Argias (Leisure Hours). Athens: Estias, 1931. Contains four
   sketches: "Contradictions of Loneliness," "Lady on a Train,"
   "Incompatibility of Character," and "Letter to a Provincial Girl."
Argo: To Xekinima (Argo: The Beginning, Part I). Athens: 1933.
   Novel.
Argo. Athens, 1936. Definitive edition in one volume. Published by
   Methuen (1951) in a translation by Ares Tsatsopoulos and E.
   Margaret Brooke. Novel.
Euripides Pendozalis and Other Stories. Athens: Pyrsos, 1937. Con-
   tains the following short fiction besides the title story: "The-
   rapeia," "The Gang," "The Garden with the Cypresses," "The
   Lake," "Her Name was Simone," "Everything's in Order,"
   "Voyage to the Island of Chimera," "Westminister," "The Man
   who wrote a Book," and "Chronicle of 1922."
To Daimonio (The Daemon). Athens: 1938. Novella.
Leonis. Athens: Pyrsos, 1940. (For the publishing history, see Chap-
   ter 4, fn. 6.) Novella.
Iera Odos (The Sacred Road). Athens: 1950. Novel.
Astheneis kai Odoiporoi (Invalids and Wayfarers). Athens: Estias,
   1964. Two volume novel.
I Kambanes (The Bells). Athens: Estias, 1970. This novella was first
   published serially, in 25 installments, in *Vima* from Dec. 4, 1966
   to Jan. 1, 1967.

2. Drama

To Yefiri tis Artas (The Bridge of Arta). Published in *Nea Estia*, vol.
   33, 1943.
Pefti to Vradi (Night Falls). *Nea Estia*, vol. 34, 1943.
Theater I, 1944. Collection contains *Night Falls, Andara st' Anapli*
   (Revolt at Anapli), *The Bridge of Arta*, and *To Oneiro tou De-
   kaimerou* (The Dream of the Twelfth Night).

To Kastro tis Orias (The Castle of the Beauty). *Nea Estia*, vol. 36, 1944.

Vyzantini Nichta (Byzantine Night). Later called *I Lakaina* (The Lacedaemonian Woman). *Nea Estia*, vol. 39, 1946.

Theater II, 1947. Collection contains *The Game of Folly vs. Virtue* and *The Castle of the Beauty*. The former play appears in English translation as *The Game of Folly vs. Wisdom* in *Introduction to Modern Greek Literature* by Mary Gianos. New York: Twayne, 1969, pp. 320–67.

Sinapandima stin Pendeli (Encounter on Pendeli). Athens: 1958.

To Timima tis Lefterias–Katsandonis (The Price of Freedom). Athens: 1958.

Sklires Rizes (Hard Roots). *Nea Estia*, vol. 65, 1959.

Alcibiades, 1959. Published in English translation in *Thespis*, a quarterly edited by the Greek Center of the International Theater Institute, June, 1966, nos. 4–5.

I Akri tou Dromou (The End of the Road). Athens: Fexis, 1963.

Theatrical Works, I: Neoelliniko Laïko Theatro. Athens: Estias, 1965. Collection contains *Revolt at Anapli, The Bridge of Arta, The Dream of the Twelfth Night, The Castle of the Beauty, The Game of Folly vs. Virtue, Encounter on Pendeli* and *The Price of Freedom*.

The Last War. Epoches, no. 25, 1965.

Theatrical Works, II: Erga Diafora. Athens: Estias, 1966. Collection contains *Night Falls, Alcibiades, The Last War, The Lacedaemonian Woman, Hard Roots* and *The End of the Road*.

3.   Verse

Phylla Imerologiou (Journal Leaves). Athens: Kastalia, April, 1934. Eighty copies printed, numbered, and circulated noncommercially. The collection contains seven poems: "The Dance Dies," "Poetic,"* "Prose Image," "Afar,"* "History," "Harmony,"* and "The Dance Begins Again."*

Journal Leaves, II. Athens: Estias, October, 1934. Fifty copies printed, numbered and circulated noncommercially. Collection contains five poems: "Vision," Loneliness,"* "To a Madonna of Sandro Botticelli,"* "Paris Night,"* and "The Old Eagle."*

Poemata tou Mesopolemou (Poems of the Midwar). Athens: Ikaros, 1944. Collection contains fourteen poems, eight in the two volumes of *Journal Leaves* indicated by asterisks and the following six: "Scientism," "Athenian Evening," "The Dead City," "The Grave of President Venizelos," "The Critical Hour," and "The Lament of the Drowned."

4. Discursive Prose

A. Separate Publications: Books and/or Pamphlets

Elefthero Pnevma (Free Spirit). Athens: Rallis, 1929. Published under the pseudonym of Orestes Digenis. Essay.

Embros sto Koinoniko Provlima (Forward to the Social Problem). Athens: 1932. Essay.

Notebook of Argo and of The Daemon. Athens: Pyrsos, 1939. Journal entries.

Sto Katofli ton Neon Kairon (On the Threshold of a New Era. Athens: Ikaros, 1945.

Dokimio gia tin Ameriki (Essay on America). Athens: Ikaros, 1954. Travel impressions.

Provlimata tou Kairou mas (Problems of Our Time). Athens: Ikaros, 1956. Contains six essays: "The Contemporary Greeks," "The Greek Writer," "Entering Politics," "The Worldly Life as a Social Phenomenon," "Advice of a Father in Our Time," and "Turbulent Years."

Journey to the Near East and Mount Athos. Athens: Fexis, 1961. Travel impressions.

Pnevmatiki Poreia (Intellectual Journey). Athens: Fexis, 1961. Works that this collection contains are too numerous to describe in detail. Briefly, it comprises "On the Threshold of a New Era," "The Ideological Crisis of our Epoch," "Return to the Roots," "General Makriyiannis," "Psycharis," "Palamas," "Cavafy," "Dragoumis," "Sikelianos," "Our Language," and "The Life of Letters." Published for the first time is "Message about Happiness."

The National Crisis. Athens: Themelio, 1966. Articles written for *Vima* concerning the political crisis that began in July, 1965. For supplementary bibliography of works on political crisis see entries from *Vima* (1966) in "periodical publications."

Travels: Persia, Roumania, Soviet Union, Bulgaria. Athens: Estias, 1971. Travel impressions gathered from *Vima* and *Epoches.* Published posthumously.

B. Periodical Publications

"Clarity [of Style]." *Kyklos* I, no. 1 (Nov., 1931), 24–30.

"Toward Unity [of the Balkan and Near Eastern Peoples]." *Idea* I, no. 1 (Jan., 1933), 13–17.

"Review of Kostas Varnalis's *The Light that Sears.*" *Idea* I, no. 2 (Feb., 1933), 101–07.

"A Disastrous Misstep [of D. Glinos]. *Idea* I, no. 4 (April, 1933), 253–57.

"Freedom and Force." *Idea* I, no. 5 (May, 1933), 281–90.

"Impressions of Yugoslavia," in two parts. *Idea* I, no. 8 (Aug., 1933), 65–69 and no. 9 (Sept., 1933), 135–39.

"Something Rotten in Greece." *Idea* I, no. 10 (Oct., 1933), 199–201.

"The New Literature [following the 1922 Disaster]." *Idea* II, no. 13 (Jan., 1934), pp. 11–17.

"The Persecution of Demoticism." *Nea Grammata* I, nos. 7–8 (July–Aug., 1935), 443–45.

"Social Issues, I, II, III, IV." *Nea Grammata* II, no. 1 (Jan., 1936) 72–74; no. 3 (March, 1936) 252–55; no. 4 (April, 1936) 339–43; and nos. 7–8 (July, 1936) 718–25.

"C. G. Karyotakis." *Neoellinika Grammata*, March 19, 1938, pp. 1–2.

"Some Questions of Modern Greek Psychology." First published in English translation in *The Link*, Oxford, June, 1938, then published in the original Greek in *Anglo-Elliniki Epitheorisi* I, no. 5 (July, 1945), 5–6.

"The Issue of Greekness of Spirit and of Art." *Neoellinika Grammata*, Dec. 17, 1938, pp. 1–2.

"The Pyrgi of Chios." *Neoellinika Grammata*, Sept. 30, 1939, pp. 1–3.

"Progressive Thoughts." *Nea Grammata* VII, no. 3 (May, 1944), 235–37.

"Theater and the Time." *Nea Estia* 39, no. 449 (March 15, 1946), 356–57.

"The First Postwar Period of the National Theater." *Nea Estia* 39; no. 451 (April 15, 1946), 460–73.

"What is Contemporary Hellenism?" *Nea Estia* 42, no. 485 (Sept. 15, 1947), 1107–10.

"The Accusatory Spirit." *Nea Estia* 43, no. 495 (Feb. 15, 1948), 207–10.

"The Future of the Greek Cinema." *Nea Estia* 46, no. 531, (Aug. 15, 1949), 1031–32.

"The Performances of Ancient Drama in Greece." *Nea Estia* 50, no. 584 (Nov. 1, 1951), 1420–22.

"Theater and Criticism." *Nea Estia* 51, no. 596 (May 1, 1952).

"The Form of Chios." *Nea Estia*, Christmas Issue, 1955, pp. 334–35.

"The Moral Problem of the Russian Revolution." *Nea Estia* 62, no. 728 (Nov. 1, 1957), 1525–26.

"Theater in Contemporary Greece." *Nea Estia* 65, no. 758, (Feb. 1, 1959), 168–77. A speech delivered at the Institute for Balkan Studies, Thessaloniki, on April 1, 1958.

"The Dramatic Theater of Modern Greece." *Twelve Lectures*, series

I, no. 1. Athens: National Theater Organization, 1961, pp. 19–37. This volume is the first in which is published a series of lectures delivered between Jan. 16 and April 17, 1961 in the Hall of the Royal Theater.

"The Art of the Novel." *Epoches*, no. 20 (Dec., 1964), pp. 6–12.

"The Constitution in the Demotic." Review of Ch. Christides's translation of the Greek Constitution. *Vima*, Nov. 28, 1965, pp. 1–5.

"Hopes and Dangers." *Vima*, Jan. 27, 1966, p. 1. This article and those that follow are in the series of political essays whose first part was published by Themelio as *The National Crisis*.

"The Dictatorship." *Vima*, Feb. 20, 1966, pp. 1–6.

"The National Idea." *Vima*, March 25, 1966, p. 1.

"The Church in our Time." *Vima*, April 10, 1966, pp. 1–6.

"What Democracy Means." *Vima*, May 29, 1966, pp. 1–6.

"The 'No' of July 15." *Vima*, July 10, 1966, p. 1.

"A Symptom of Illness." *Vima*, Oct. 8, 1966, p. 1.

"Ideas and Persons." *Vima*, Oct. 15, 1966, p. 1.

SECONDARY SOURCES

ANONYMOUS. "Interview with George Theotokas." *Elefthera Grammata* I, no. 17 (Aug. 31, 1945), 3–4.

ANONYMOUS. "Interview with George Theotokas." *Vima*, Jan. 21, 1965, p. 2.

ANONYMOUS. "Interview with George Theotokas on the occasion of the publication of *Neoelliniko Laïko Theatro*." *Vima*, Dec. 19, 1965, p. 9.

ANONYMOUS. "Prose; Movements, Influences, the Climate—An Interview with George Theotokas." *Epitheorisi Technis*, March, 1966, pp. 180–81.

ANONYMOUS. "Interview with George Theotokas on occasion of the publication of *The National Crisis*." *Vima*, Feb. 9, 1966, p. 2.

ANONYMOUS. "George Theotokas: Genos, Biographika." *Chiaki Epitheorisi* V, no. 13 (1967), 1–4.

ANTONIADOU, SOPHIA. "Review of *Argo: The Beginning*." *Idea* I, no. 12, (Dec., 1933), 375–78.

————. "New Currents in Modern Greek Literature, from 1922 and after." *Nea Estia* 46, nos. 531–32 (Aug. 15–Sept. 1, 1949), 1034–40; 1125–30.

APOSTOLIDIS, RENOS. "Review of *The Sacred Road*." In *Kritiki to Metapolemou*, Athens, 1962. Pp. 156–70.

ARGYRIOU, ALEX. "George Theotokas: His Intellectual Presence in Greek Letters." *Epitheorisi Technis*, no. 146 (Feb., 1967), pp. 118–30.

DARZENTA, IRENE. "The Drama of Theotokas," *Zenon*, Piraeus, April 1963, Vol. IV, No. 28, pp. 113–19.

DECAVALLES, ANDONIS, ed. with LEE HATFIELD. "George Theotokas: A Critical Mosaic," with comments by I. M. Panayotopoulos, Andreas Karandonis and Apostolos Sachinis, *The Charioteer*, No. 5, 1963, pp. 60–64.

DIMARAS, CONSTANTINE TH. "Review of *On the Threshold*." *Vima*, Jan. 6, 1946, pp. 1–2.

—————. "George Theotokas: An Obituary." *Vima*, Nov. 25, 1966, pp. 1–2.

—————. "George Theotokas and *The Free Spirit*." Introduction to *The Free Spirit*. Athens: Hermes, 1973.

FAFALIOS, K. D. "George Theotokas: An Appreciation." *Chiaki Epitheorisi* V, no. 13 (1967), 5–9.

FRANGOPOULOS, TH. D. "George Theotokas," *Tachydromos*, no. 662, Dec. 17, 1966, pp. 74–75.

GIALOURAKIS, MANOLIS. "George Theotokas." *Megale Enkyklopaidia Neoellinikis Logotechnias*, vol. VII, pp. 111–13. Athens: Haris Patzis, 1968.

HATZIANESTIS, ERRIKOS. "Review of *Invalids and Wayfarers*." *Epoches*, no. 15, (July, 1964), pp. 67–70.

HATZINIS, YIANNIS. "Review of *Intellectual Journey*." *Nea Estia* vol. 71, no. 830 (Feb. 1, 1962), 203–205.

HOURMOUZIOS, AIMILIOS. "Modern Greek Literature between Two Wars," *Ilios Enkyklopaidia*, vol. VII, pp. 1113–17.

KARANDONIS, ANDREAS. "George Theotokas." In *Prose Writers and Prose Works of the Generation of the Thirties*. Athens: Fexis, 1962. Pp. 64–127.

KUBLY, HERBERT. *Gods and Heroes*. London: Gollancz, 1970.

LAIMOS, ANDREAS. "About George Theotokas." *Chiaki Epitheorisi* V, no. 13 (1967) 10–14. From a speech delivered at the Philotechnikos Omilos of Chios on Dec. 18, 1966.

LAMBRAKIS, CHRISTOS. "George Theotokas and Engaged Thought." *Epoches*, 45 (Jan., 1966), pp. 7–10.

MACKRIDGE, PETER. "Bibliography of George Theotokas and Kosmas Politis." *Mantatophoros*, Bulletin of Modern Greek Studies, Issue 3, Nov., 1973, pp. 17–20.

MATSAS, NESTOR. "Interview with George Theotokas." *Nea Estia* 51, no. 589 (Jan. 15, 1952), 131–33.

MERAKLIS, M. G. *Contemporary Greek Literature, 1945–1970*, II. Prose. Thessaloniki, 1972.

MOULLAS, PANAGIOTIS. "George Theotokas and the Essay." *Epitheorisi Technis*, March, 1966, pp. 182–87.

MYLONOYIANNIS, G. M. "Review of *The Daemon.*" *Neoellinika Grammata*, Oct. 22, 1938, pp. 14–15.

PANAYOTOPOULOS, I. M. "George Theotokas." In *Persons and Texts*, II, "Uneasy Years." Athens: Aetos, 1943.

PERASTIKOS, G. "Portrait of George Theotokas." *Neoellinika Grammata*, Nov. 20, 1937, pp. 12–14.

PLASKOVITIS, SPYROS. "George Theotokas." *Epoches*, 45 (Jan., 1966), pp. 11–14.

PORPHYRIS, K. "Review of *The National Crisis.*" *Epitheorisi Technis*, March, 1966, pp. 295–97.

SACHINIS, APOSTOLOS. "The Novel of Adolescence." In *I Synchroni Pezographia Mas* (Our Contemporary Fiction). Athens: Ikaros, 1951. Discussion of Leonis is on pp. 31–34.

—————. "Review of *Journey to the Middle East and Mount Athos* and *Invalids and Wayfarers.*" in *Pezographoi tou Kairou mas* (Prose Writers of our Time). Athens: Estias, 1967. Pp. 115–21.

SEFERIS, GEORGE. "Discussion with Fabrizio." *Epoches*, 45 (Jan., 1966), pp. 3–6.

SKOULOUDIS, MANOLIS. "Interview with George Theotokas." *Neoellinika Grammata*, Sept. 15, 1935, p. 3.

SPANDONIDIS, PETROS. *I Pezographia ton Neon* (The Prose of the Young, 1929–1933). Thessaloniki, 1934.

THRYLOS, ALKIS. "George Theotokas, The Climate of Intellectual Play and Virtue." *Nea Estia* 53, no. 617 (March 15, 1953), 365–68 and no. 618 (April 1, 1953), pp. 469–73.

VENEZIS, ILIAS. "The Generation of the 1930s: At the Home of Theotokas." *Vima*, March 12, 1963, pp. 1–2.

VITTI, MARIO. *Due generazione di romanzieri greci, 1920–1950.* Palermo: 1970.

Index

(The works of Theotokas are listed under his name)

181